Second Sino-Japanese War

A Captivating Guide to a Military Conflict Primarily Waged Between China and Japan and the Rape of Nanking

© Copyright 2021

All Rights Reserved. No part of this book may be reproduced in any form without permission in writing from the author. Reviewers may quote brief passages in reviews.

Disclaimer: No part of this publication may be reproduced or transmitted in any form or by any means, mechanical or electronic, including photocopying or recording, or by any information storage and retrieval system, or transmitted by email without permission in writing from the publisher.

While all attempts have been made to verify the information provided in this publication, neither the author nor the publisher assumes any responsibility for errors, omissions or contrary interpretations of the subject matter herein.

This book is for entertainment purposes only. The views expressed are those of the author alone, and should not be taken as expert instruction or commands. The reader is responsible for his or her own actions.

Adherence to all applicable laws and regulations, including international, federal, state and local laws governing professional licensing, business practices, advertising and all other aspects of doing business in the US, Canada, UK or any other jurisdiction is the sole responsibility of the purchaser or reader.

Neither the author nor the publisher assumes any responsibility or liability whatsoever on the behalf of the purchaser or reader of these materials. Any perceived slight of any individual or organization is purely unintentional.

Free Bonus from Captivating History (Available for a Limited time)

Hi History Lovers!

Now you have a chance to join our exclusive history list so you can get your first history ebook for free as well as discounts and a potential to get more history books for free! Simply visit the link below to join.

Captivatinghistory.com/ebook

Also, make sure to follow us on Facebook, Twitter and Youtube by searching for Captivating History.

Table of Contents

PART 1: THE SECOND SINO-JAPANESE WAR 1

    INTRODUCTION TO ONE OF THE WORLD'S BLOODIEST CONFLICTS 2

    CHAPTER 1 – THE ROOTS OF THE CONFLICT 4

    CHAPTER 2 – JAPAN BEFORE THE WAR 21

    CHAPTER 3 – MANCHURIA/MANCHUKUO 27

    CHAPTER 4 – CHINA PROPER 38

    CHAPTER 5 – ANOTHER "INCIDENT" 41

    CHAPTER 6 – THE OPPONENTS 52

    CHAPTER 7 – THE TRAGEDY OF NANJING 71

    CHAPTER 8 – THEY WERE EXPENDABLE 80

    CHAPTER 9 – THE WAR DRAGS ON 84

    CHAPTER 10 – HORRORS MOSTLY UNKNOWN 89

    CHAPTER 11 – FRIENDS 96

    CONCLUSION – THE END OF THE WAR 105

PART 2: THE RAPE OF NANKING 109

    INTRODUCTION 110

    CHAPTER 1 – A QUICK HISTORY OF SINO-JAPANESE RELATIONS ... 113

    CHAPTER 2 – A BRIEF HISTORY OF NANJING 121

    CHAPTER 3 – JAPAN'S INVASION OF CHINA 126

    CHAPTER 4 – THE SECOND BATTLE OF SHANGHAI AND
    BUILDING FRUSTRATION AND RESENTMENT TOWARD THE
    CHINESE 133

    CHAPTER 5 – WAR CRIMES COMMITTED ON THE WAY TO
    NANJING 141

    CHAPTER 6 – THE ORDER TO KILL 146

    CHAPTER 7 – DEFENDING AGAINST THE IMPOSSIBLE 149

    CHAPTER 8– NANJING'S DISORGANIZATION AND FAILED
    PREPARATIONS 153

    CHAPTER 9 – NANJING FALLS 158

    CHAPTER 10 – A CONTEST TO KILL AND THE EXECUTION OF
    CHINESE PRISONERS OF WAR 165

    CHAPTER 11 – THE RAPE OF TENS OF THOUSANDS OF PEOPLE 170

    CHAPTER 12 – MASS KILLINGS AND DESECRATION OF THE
    DEAD 174

    CHAPTER 13 – STEALING THE VALUABLES AND DESTROYING
    THE CITY 178

    CHAPTER 14 – REPORTS OF THE RAPES AND ATROCITIES
    REACH THE GENERALS AND INVESTIGATIONS BEGIN 181

    CHAPTER 15 – DECLARING THE RESTORATION OF ORDER 187

    CHAPTER 16 – WANG CHING-WEI, THE PUPPET GOVERNMENT,
    AND THE END OF THE WAR 190

    CHAPTER 17 – THE NANJING WAR CRIMES TRIBUNAL AND
    JOHN RABE'S LIFE AFTER THE EVENTS IN NANJING 199

    CHAPTER 18 – THE MEMORIAL HALL OF THE VICTIMS IN
    NANJING 206

CHAPTER 19 - HOW THE ATROCITIES WERE REPORTED AND
RESULTING CONTROVERSIES 209

CONCLUSION 216

HERE'S ANOTHER BOOK BY CAPTIVATING HISTORY THAT YOU
MIGHT LIKE 218

FREE BONUS FROM CAPTIVATING HISTORY (AVAILABLE FOR A
LIMITED TIME) 219

SOURCES.. 220

Part 1: The Second Sino-Japanese War

A Captivating Guide to Military Conflict That Began between China and Japan, Including Events Such as the Japanese Invasion of Manchuria and the Nanjing Massacre

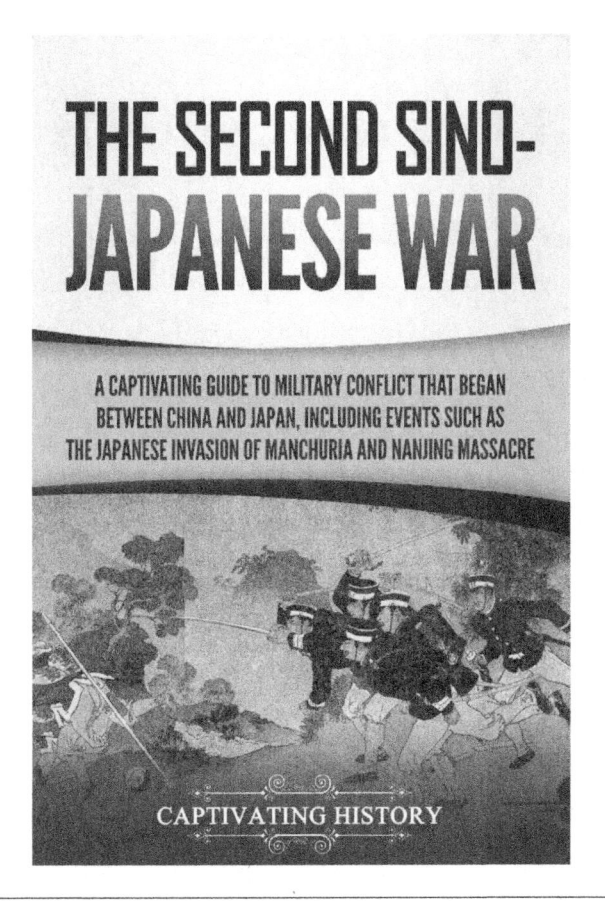

Introduction to One of the World's Bloodiest Conflicts

For most people in Europe, World War II began in 1939 with the German invasion of Poland. Those in the territories of the Soviet Union (conveniently forgetting the Soviet invasion of Finland and eastern Poland in 1939) mark the start of the "Great Patriotic War" as June 22nd, 1941, when Hitler's armies attacked their country. Most Americans mark the beginning of the war as December 7th, 1941, with the attack on Pearl Harbor by the Japanese. It's all a matter of perspective.

Circle around the world to Asia, however, and you get an entirely different point of view. Academic historians differ in their opinions, but they usually fall into two camps regarding the start of World War II in Asia: either 1931, with the Japanese invasion of Manchuria, a remote semi-autonomous region of China at the time, or 1936, when the Japanese invaded China proper. In either case, the war in Asia went on far longer than the war in Europe, and it likely cost just as many lives, with most of them being Chinese.

Many people in the West look upon the Second Sino-Japanese War, which took place in the 1930s and 1940s, as a sort of sideshow to the larger Second World War, but there is no separating the two. Imagine the Pacific War, the theater of World War II that took place in the Pacific. If the Japanese were not busy fighting on another front, they would have had millions of more troops available to fight the Americans and the British. In all likelihood, World War II would have ended the same way, but it would have taken much longer and cost that many more lives.

To understand the conflict between these two Asian powers, we have to travel back in time quite a ways, for the story of what is known by many as the Second Sino-Japanese War is long and rooted deep in history.

Chapter 1 – The Roots of the Conflict

In China, the war with Japan is called by a variety of names, including the official "Fourteen Years' War of Resistance," with it being referred to as the "Eight Years' War of Resistance" earlier on, and it is also sometimes referred to as part of the "Global Anti-Fascist War," which, of course, it was.

In today's Japan, the war is most often referred to as the "Japan-China War," but when the war actually began, the Japanese government referred to it as the "North China Incident." That changed shortly thereafter when Japan invaded Shanghai, and the war became known as simply the "China Incident," which was clearly an understatement. The word "incident" resulted partially as a result of there being no formal declaration of war and also due to Japan's desire to downplay their actions to the international audience.

Even today, when it is clear to almost everyone who was to blame for the war in China, some Japanese, within the government and without, call the war the "Japan-China Incident. This "incident" cost upward of twenty million lives.

When World War II broke out in the Pacific, the war in China became the "Greater East Asia War," which was far more accurate, as the conflict was fought over thousands of miles and involved, in one way or another, China, Japan, the United States, Great Britain, India, and the Soviet Union.

To understand the *Second* Sino-Japanese War, we need to go back to the *First* Sino-Japanese War. However, to understand that war, we need to go back a bit further to examine how the two countries got to that point. Of course, what happened in the centuries before the Second Sino-Japanese War does not bear directly on our subject, but that does not mean it did not have some effect.

Roots

Historians and now genetic ethnologists (those who study the genetic roots of peoples and their migrations) tell us that Japan was originally populated by the Jomon people, a distinct ethnic group that still lives on in the DNA of the Ainu, a people who live in the northern areas of Japan, predominantly on the northern island of Hokkaido, and who are distinctly different from most Japanese. These people are related to many of the indigenous peoples of northern Asia and distantly with the native peoples of North America.

People from the Asian mainland, known as the Yayoi, migrated to Japan and intermingled with the native groups already there; simply put, this resulted in the modern Japanese. This all took place approximately from 300 BCE to 300 CE. Over time, a unique Japanese culture was born.

There are many things at which the Japanese excel, and one of them is absorbing and adapting foreign technologies and cultures into their own. For the first few centuries after their arrival, the Yayoi people, who eventually formed into the modern Japanese, imported much of their culture from the Asian mainland. This included their system of writing, religious and philosophical beliefs, and even clothing and court habits. As time went by, these were changed to fit what was becoming a unique and geographically isolated culture. Chinese characters became Japanese, and ideas such as Buddhism underwent changes and became unique to Japan, for example, Zen Buddhism.

For many centuries, the Japanese led relatively isolated lives. Of course, there was trade done with China and the Asian mainland (mostly Korea), and Japan became dependent on China for many things, such as the expensive silk that was used in the clothing of the upper class, namely for kimonos.

You would think, given such a long history, that the Japanese and Chinese would have warred against each other many times over the centuries, but that was not what happened. For the Chinese, Japan was a backwater country, and besides, it was located over the ocean. Trade with Japan was but one small part of their economy, as China had a much more lucrative trade with the West (namely with the kingdoms of the Middle East and later Europe) and to the south, with India and the tributary states of Southeast Asia.

For Japan's part, much of the early history of the country was spent at war with itself. The rise of the samurai class and their warrior ethos took place around the 900s, and these thoughts and practices only increased. Rival clans and alliances spent decades or more at war, as they attempted to unite the country under one man (or one family), or some smaller variation on a more local scale.

It was not until the late 13th century that the national forces of both countries faced each other on the battlefield. This was the attempted invasion of Japan by the Mongols, who had taken over China in the previous decades.

The Mongols, whose army was made up of not only of Mongolians but of Chinese and Koreans, attempted to conquer Japan twice, in 1274 and 1281. A huge Mongol/Chinese fleet (the ships themselves were commanded and mostly manned by ethnic Chinese, as the Mongols were nomadic horse warriors from the Asian steppes, far from any ocean) appeared off the northwestern coast of the southernmost Japanese island, Kyushu, in 1274 after the demands by the Mongol emperor, Kublai Khan, had been rejected. He had been *firmly* rejected, too—his envoys were decapitated, and their heads were sent back to China.

Though the Mongols gained a small foothold in their first attempt, they were thwarted both times by storms, which destroyed many of their ships and forced them to retreat due to the lack of supplies. In both invasions, warriors from both sides encountered each other frequently, though many believe the storms prevented any real fighting. In the first case, Mongol mass tactics seem to have gotten the upper hand for a time, as opposed to the samurai tactic of fighting individual "honorable" battles. By the time of the second invasion, the Japanese had built up considerable defenses and met the Mongols, this time not only with different tactics but also with an early type of special forces raid, in which men swam to the Mongol fleet and set many ships ablaze.

After these two costly attempts, Kublai Khan and his descendants, while still claiming Japan as theirs, gave up on any attempts at conquering the island nation. As you might realize, the storms that brewed up both times to help defeat the Mongols were referred to by the Japanese as winds sent by their gods to protect them; they were called "divine winds," or *kamikaze*.

For over the next six centuries, Japan and China lived side by side in relative peace, though pirates from both sides (and sometimes even in united teams) preyed upon the coasts and coastal shipping lanes of both countries.

In the late 16th century, a new force had entered Asian power politics. These were the Europeans, who came from various nations, including Spain, Portugal, Holland, and England. During the European "Age of Discovery," seafarers from Europe went out in search of a faster route to the riches of Asia. By crossing the seas rather than the vast lands of the Middle and Far East, they hoped to avoid not only the dangers of hostile bandits, clans, and nations but also the taxes and tolls of those in power. The Europeans were the first to sail the open oceans in any serious numbers, and their hope was that they could find an easier route to China and India and the riches they believed and knew were there: jewels, gold, silk, and spices, all of which had been traded throughout the centuries over the vast lands of the "Silk Road" that had been described by Marco Polo and others.

The reactions of Japan and China to the Europeans were different from each other, with the size of their nations playing a role. China, one of the largest nations/kingdoms on Earth, was hard to police, especially when dynasties were falling and local warlords took power away from the capital. In many cases, the Europeans moved in and played one warlord against another for trade rights. By the early 19th century, the ruling dynasty in China, the Qing, was beginning to weaken, and with the arrival of Western military forces and their advanced technology, the government began to make concessions to various European nations in the hopes of avoiding conflicts that they probably could not win.

In contrast, Japan, by the late 1500s/early 1600s, had been unified by one man and family, the Tokugawa clan, whose first ruler, Tokugawa Ieyasu, had become shōgun ("barbarian conquering general") in 1600. By the time of his death in 1616, Tokugawa Ieyasu had effectively banned all foreigners from Japan, except for a small area around the southern city of Hiroshima. All Japanese were banned from traveling abroad as well. Among his many missions, protecting the unique nature of Japan from the outside was paramount. This policy of isolation continued until the 1850s, when the Americans, under threat of force, opened Japan up to increased foreign trade and personnel. Still, the Japanese, especially after the restoration of imperial power in 1868, kept the foreigners under strict supervision and deftly played one Western power against another.

Tokugawa Ieyasu had bought weapons from the Europeans, but he did not allow them inside his country, which the Chinese did, to their detriment. In all fairness, many factors contributed to the decline of Chinese power in the early 1800s, among them a weakening of the ruling Qing dynasty, which grew more and more corrupt as time went by. Between 1839 to 1842, the Chinese fought the First Opium War against the British. Simply put, the British, who had secured a virtual monopoly on the opium trade in India and the Middle East, wished to sell opium in China. For their part, the Chinese had been fighting against opium addiction for some time and did not want the British selling opium in their country. The trade was so lucrative for the British, though, that they were willing to go to war with China to force the Chinese to allow British opium in the country. This war resulted in a humiliating defeat for the Chinese, who were outgunned and outmatched and defeated by the significantly smaller forces of the British.

The First Opium War had resulted in the Chinese being forced to open five treaty ports, which allowed Britain to virtually control the economic activity within them, and ceding Hong Kong Island to Great Britain. Still, after the first war, the Chinese did what they could to stymie the efforts of the British and other Western powers, who pushed not only for the enforcement of their "rights" secured after the first war but also more access to trade within China, especially in, you guessed it, opium.

Depiction of battle between British and Chinese troops during the Second Opium War
https://commons.wikimedia.org/wiki/File:Capture_of_the_Peiho_Forts.jpg

In between the two wars, there were many incidents of Chinese mobs assaulting Europeans, whom many saw as invaders and thieves. In retaliation, the British and French forces often retaliated or demanded the Chinese government hand over their nationals for trial in British or French courts. Foreigners trying one's citizens in their own country according to foreign laws are usually grounds for war, even today. However, from the European perspective at the time, many Chinese were "let off the hook," and what the British saw as "free trade" was blocked by the Chinese whenever they could.

The Second Opium War was fought between 1856 and 1860, which was about ten years after the First Opium War, and it pitted China against both Britain and France. Once again, the Chinese were defeated, and further concessions were granted to the Europeans. Within China, many people were angry not only at the Europeans but also at their government, which they began to see as weak and incompetent.

As the 19th century wore on, more and more European powers, including Russia, Germany, Belgium, Italy, and Holland, demanded the same economic rights in China as the British and French. By the 1890s, many of these powers had what were called "concessions" in Chinese cities on the coast. This effectively meant that at least in part of these cities, foreigners controlled the trade, taxes, and even who lived where. In reality, Chinese trade with the outside world was controlled by foreign powers.

Two powers came late to the "game," the United States and Japan. Though the US attempted to initiate a somewhat fairer Chinese trade policy among the world powers (known as the Open Door policy), the truth is that American companies moved in and attempted to get their "fair share" of the Chinese market themselves. Additionally, though the Europeans had begun to bring in Christian missionaries to China, it wasn't until the arrival of the Americans that Christianity began to slowly spread in China. For the most part, it only caused more resentment.

Japan, which between 1868 and the 1890s had become the most technologically advanced country in Asia, saw the opportunities in China, as well as the European gains not only in China but also in all of Asia, and wanted a "piece of the pie" itself.

Japan's move to become a world power began in Korea, which was, at the time, a united kingdom that was sometimes referred to as a hermit kingdom due to its isolation from the rest of the world.

For centuries, Korea had been a client state of China, providing tribute and much coal and iron. With Japan's growing modern technology, much of it dependent on exactly that, it saw Korea as a prime target for its growing military power. Requests and demands that China open Korea to Japanese trade were rebuffed, and so, Japan used this as an excuse to go to war with China. The ensuing conflict, the First Sino-Japanese War, was fought for about nine months between 1894 to 1895, and it resulted in another Chinese defeat. This gave Japan control of Korea, which it absorbed and colonized, and Japan also forced China to cede Taiwan to them. Japan also demanded the same rights within Chinese coastal cities as the Europeans and Americans had.

Between 1899 and 1901, Japanese forces joined with European forces to help put down the Chinese anti-foreigner Boxer Rebellion. This, in turn, gave Japan more concessions within China. The Boxer Rebellion was noted for its atrocities on both sides, as Chinese mobs and militias killed and tortured foreign soldiers and also raped foreign women that fell into their hands. For their part, the German, Russian, and Japanese troops became known for their ruthlessness in response, particularly the Japanese, who frequently burned entire villages alive in retaliation.

Troops of the "8-Nation Army" during the time of the Boxer Rebellion. From left to right: Britain, USA, Australia, British India, Germany, Austria-Hungary, Italy, and Japan
https://commons.wikimedia.org/wiki/File:Troops_of_the_Eight_nations_alliance_1900.jpg

The First Sino-Japanese War also put Japan on a collision course with another country, Russia, which bordered both China and Korea. Disputes over sea boundaries, as well as disputes over which nation should control areas in and near Korea, as well as Manchuria, the huge resource-rich northernmost province of China, arose. Control of sea lanes often meant control of the countries and/or their economies.

The world expected the Russians to soundly defeat the Japanese. These reasons included Russia's vast size, what was believed to be its superior military power (especially at sea), and racist ideas that the smaller Japanese could not possibly defeat Europeans in the field. Of course, you don't have to be large to fire a gun.

Between 1904 and 1905, the Russo-Japanese War took place, and it resulted in the Japanese defeating the Russian Empire. A treaty brokered by US President Theodore Roosevelt ended the war, which gave Japan many more rights and privileges in northern China and Manchuria. It also weakened Russian power and allowed Japan to join the European nations as a world power.

The division of coastal Chinese cities into concessions, the ceding of Taiwan, Hong Kong Island, and other territories (such as Macao), and the foreign control over much of China's economy weakened China greatly. Of course, it also caused great resentment within the country. Over the next three decades, both the nationalist and communist movements within China would try to harness this resentment and turn it into political power, but until the communist victory of 1949, they were not successful—in fact, they were quite the opposite.

For many years, various movements within China, on either a local or national level, had been working to either reform or overthrow the Qing dynasty, which had ruled China with varying degrees of effectiveness since 1644. Starting with the defeats in the Opium Wars, many people within

China began to believe that the Qing were losing the "Mandate of Heaven," which is the traditional Chinese belief that a regime came to power because the gods willed or allowed it. Conversely, when the regime lost the support of the gods, those supernatural beings withdrew their support, meaning that rocky times were indeed ahead. Once the majority of the population began to wonder if a dynasty had lost the Mandate of Heaven, it was likely that its end was drawing near.

By the early 20th century, the Qing, in many ways, ruled only in name. The nation was divided into literal fiefdoms, where local strongmen, better known to history as "warlords," held most of the power. Some of these men presided over quite small territories. Others, like General Yuan Shikai, ruled over entire provinces and millions of people; these leaders were national figures and power brokers, but most of them were also quite corrupt.

So were many of the rulers of the Qing dynasty. By the end of the dynasty in 1912, really nothing of any import had been accomplished in China without someone, or many people, being paid off. This was made even more complicated, at least in the populous coastal areas, by the presence of the foreigners, who very frequently wanted their cut of the profits or a say in what happened.

Needless to say, China stagnated. The population (which, in 1900, was about 400 million and the most populous on Earth, just as it is today) was overwhelmingly poor. Most lived in the countryside and were peasants with very few rights, if they had any at all. Natural disasters were a regular occurrence, including locust plagues, famine, epidemics, and floods. Floods in the major river systems were sometimes responsible for the deaths of tens of thousands of people at a single time, which only led to more epidemics and misery.

Many of these disasters were naturally occurring, but in many cases, they were made worse by the lack of any type of planning or construction that might alleviate the heavy damage. Money and equipment to construct levees, as well as other such preventive measures, often fell into private hands, never to be seen again.

The peasants were also subject to ancient rules, customs, and laws that made their existence even more miserable. The eternal enemy of the average Chinese people were those of the "landlord class." Landlords were often absentee and lived hundreds of miles away, most never even seeing the lands they effectively ruled over. In their place, many landlords employed overseers, many of whom used their position not only to enrich themselves but to also abuse their positions, usually in the form of some sort of sexual abuse of wives or daughters of the peasants they oversaw.

When famine struck, and it struck with alarming regularity, landlords and local governments were supposed to have emergency stores ready. Sometimes they did, but most of the time, these food stores were sold to the highest bidder, frequently in cities miles away.

All of this, in turn, led to frequent peasant uprisings. These were usually very violent affairs, for the peasants knew that if they did not succeed, they were likely to lose their lives in the most brutal fashion. Landlords were hung, torn apart, and thrown down wells, just to name a few of the fates that awaited them. The same happened for those peasants that were punished by the local militias or thugs who were hired by the landlords to put down any sign of rebellion.

On a national level, more advanced elements of society—meaning those with money, connections, and education—formed the Kuomintang, more commonly known in English as the Chinese Nationalists. Their leader was Sun Yat-sen, who had been working toward reform and revolution since the late 1800s. Still known in China as the "Father of Modern China," Sun was trained as a doctor, but in his travels, he saw the misery of the Chinese people and the corruption of its government and became determined to change it. Becoming a revolutionary, where he traveled the nation making contacts, wrote books and pamphlets, made speeches, and raised money, Sun was frequently forced to flee for his life and ended up making his way through Britain, Japan, and Canada. In those countries, he learned, in a more personal way, the ins and outs of democratic politics, and in Japan, he learned the importance of strength to limit the influence of foreigners.

Returning to China in 1903, Sun helped to form the "United League," the first national resistance movement to the Qing. This was an important first step, but the group was only loosely aligned, and while it succeeded publicizing its goals, it failed to produce a nation-changing revolution. Sun traveled overseas again, this time to the United States as well, to raise money and gain sympathy for the Chinese people.

Sun Yat-sen
https://commons.wikimedia.org/wiki/File:Sun_Yat_Sen_portrait_2_(9to12).jpg

The Chinese relationship with the United States before World War II is an interesting one. Though the US did take part in the concessions movement in the early 1900s, it was seen by the Chinese as the "best of the worst," so to speak, and its attempts at salvaging some sort of Chinese dignity with its policies was seen in a positive light. Additionally, many thousands of American Christian missionaries came to China in the late 19th and early 20th centuries. Though many Chinese deeply resented this attempt by the people of such a young country to "educate" them as to the nature of heaven and the universe, many did embrace the new faith. Those who did not embrace it at least saw that the Americans (along with many British and Canadians) were trying to help improve the lives of the Chinese peasants through building schools, food aid, medicine, etc.

By 1911, dissatisfaction with the Qing boiled over. Charges of corruption on a major railroad project led to anger among foreigners and workers in central China, and the Qing secret police uncovered a plot by soldiers in the Wuhan province, which erupted into a mutiny that spread in army units throughout the country.

Warlord Yuan Shikai was asked by the Qing to restore order and form a new government, but he dithered, and so, the events in China outstripped any of his efforts. By 1912, Sun Yat-sen emerged as the leading figure of the anti-Qing forces and entered into talks with Yuan, who was representing the Qing government. These events eventually led to the abdication of the two-year-old emperor, Puyi (as seen in the movie *The Last Emperor*, 1987).

Sun and his allies wrote a new constitution for the nation, but since Sun was a somewhat divisive figure with a lot of foreign ties, Yuan Shikai was made president, though everyone knew that Sun was the one who held the reins of power.

One of Sun's closest allies was his relative by marriage, Chiang Kai-shek. Chiang was a scheming military man who used his position with Sun to advance his own power. His wife, Soong Mei-ling, who was even more of a schemer than Chiang, was related to Sun by marriage and had been born into the wealthy Soong family of merchants (as can be seen, in Japan, like some other Asian nations, the family name is listed first). The two of them were well placed to take power when Sun died in 1925.

Unfortunately for China, the Chinese Nationalists under Sun and others were not able to effectively rule outside of the coastal cities. In the vast hinterlands and central cities of China, warlords, who were now even more populous and powerful since the overthrow of the Qing, had vast areas of the country in their hands. Without them, the Chinese Nationalist Party could not rule at all and were forced to negotiate and compromise with warlords all over the country.

This compromise with corrupt warlords, as well as the age-old abuses previously described, resulted in the swift rise of a new party from within the ranks of the Nationalists—the Communist Party of China, which was formally founded in 1921 in Shanghai. Most of these men had been in the radical wing of the Nationalist Party for some time but had adhered to the teachings of Karl Marx of Germany and Vladimir Lenin of Russia. Believing that they could foment a communist rebellion in an agrarian peasant society (whereas Marx believed a nation needed to pass into the workers/capitalist stage for socialism/communism to have any chance of success), these men formed the Communist Party of China after becoming disillusioned by the ineffectiveness of the Kuomintang (the Chinese Nationalist Party) and the continual corruption in Chinese society. Among these men was Mao Zedong and Zhou Enlai.

Zhou Enlai and Mao Zedong, 1935
https://commons.wikimedia.org/wiki/File:1937_Mao_Zhou_Qin_in_Yan%27an.jpg

By 1927, the differences between the two parties in terms of beliefs and goals for China was so great that the Chinese Civil War erupted. The Communists received some aid from the Soviet Union but were vastly outgunned by the Kuomintang and the armies of the warlords allied with them.

The Chinese Communists had several things going for them. Firstly, unlike the Kuomintang, they were seen as free from foreign influence and corruption. Secondly, they operated in secret cells, which made destroying the Communists almost impossible. Third, the Communists operated in the countryside. For the most part, they were peasants hiding among peasants, with goals similar to the people around them. Fourth, after some hard lessons, the Communists began to carry out a guerrilla war, striking suddenly and retreating before a response could be coordinated. Lastly, the Communists had an appealing philosophy that was combined with really effective propaganda. The Chinese Communist beliefs called for rule from the bottom-up, rather than the top-down, to put it simply. Instead of slow reforms as the Nationalists preached, the Communists called for the immediate overthrow and eradication of the landlord class, and in the areas under their control in the countryside, they did just that.

By 1931, China was a divided country. War existed in fits and starts between the Communists and the Nationalists, the foreigners controlled much of the economy, and what central government did exist was forced to compromise with largely corrupt warlords who controlled their own private armies, some of them quite large. China, at this point, was not a strong country and became something of a target, and it was in 1931 that Japan decided to act against China, something that they had been planning for quite some time.

Chapter 2 – Japan before the War

The Japan of the 1920s and early 1930s was a nation at war with itself. There was not an actual civil war, such as there had been in the United States in the 1860s, but the nation was being pulled in different directions by the various political factions and cultural undercurrents, and for each action, there was an opposite reaction.

We should also not forget Japan's geographical situation and the restrictions it placed on its government and people. As you most likely know, Japan is an island chain about the size of California. In the 1930s, its population was about 65 million people, twice that and more of modern California, the most populous US state. Unlike California, however, Japan does not have a great deal of arable land to sustain its people. Even today, much of the nation's food supply must be imported. These are two reasons for the amazingly high cost of living in Japan today.

To make problems worse, the islands have virtually no coal and oil reserves, the two necessities vital for a modern nation, then as now.

Today, though Japan has found alternative power sources, it is still dependent on foreign oil, which makes it quite vulnerable.

When one looks back at history for reasons a war began, you can usually find that the nations involved all had some sort of culpability. This is even true with the Pacific War in the 1940s, but when we look at the Second Sino-Japanese War, the blame for starting the war can be laid solely on the doorstep of the Japanese. That is not to say that the Japanese did not have their reasons, which we will look at in a moment.

Japan won its first war with the Chinese in 1896. It was victorious against Russia in 1905. In World War I, Japan joined the Allies (Great Britain, France, the USA, and Italy). This was not out of a sense of kinship with these democratic powers, though Japan was ostensibly a parliamentary democracy at the time. No, Japan joined the Allies because it realized that Germany possessed some vital territories in the Pacific, as well as concessions in China, and without their navy in Asia to defend them, these territories were ripe for the picking. The Western powers were more than happy to let the Japanese handle the small German forces in Asia so as not to have to divert theirs from Europe, and anyways, on the whole, the German territories and concessions were not as valuable as those of Great Britain and France.

Within Japan, the victories in the wars of the late 19th and early 20th centuries strengthened the hand of militarists who believed that Japan's martial/samurai past could be brought back to life in the modern era. In some quarters, this militarism had more than a tinge of racism to it, especially in regard to China, whom many Japanese regarded as weak, disorganized, dirty, and relatively uncivilized. Later on, this racism would be applied to the European powers and the United States in a two-edged way: Japan gained a modicum of support from other Asian powers in stating that Europeans dominated Asia and Asians and should be kicked out. Some belonging to the right-wing in Japan also believed the Americans and British (among others) to be decadent and "soft," as they did not have the martial spirit of the samurai. It is easy to see how this led to an alliance with Nazi Germany later on. But let's not get too far ahead of ourselves.

From 1600 to 1868, Japan had been governed by the Tokugawa family. As with most dynasties, this one became weaker and more corrupt with time. By the 1860s, many in Japan saw their nation at risk of being weakened by foreign influence as the Chinese were, and they were disgusted at the wide-spread corruption in their government. On top of this, the leaders within the Tokugawa shogunate (so named for its top official, the shōgun) were keen to keep things as they were—to put it simply, in a samurai world, with limited use of modern technology.

In the 1860s, civil war erupted with Japan. By 1868, the forces who believed in restoring the emperor to his full power (rather than as the figurehead the emperor had been for centuries) won the war. Emperor Meiji (b.1852-d. 1912), while ruling with the advice of a parliament, had full and complete power. This period in Japanese history is known as the Meiji Restoration, and it symbolizes not only the return of the emperor to power but also a period of time in Japanese history where it was virtually unparalleled in its growth and modernization until the present day.

Meiji's son, Emperor Taishō, was not anywhere the equal of his father. During his reign from 1912 to 1926, others fought for the power that Emperor Taishō had, as he did not seem to be overly concerned with having it. Emperor Taishō had other problems, mainly a host of physical ailments that preoccupied his time and limited his abilities. Most of these problems were neurological, but the emperor suffered from a host of other issues as well, such as a serious lack of charisma and an inability to articulate well, which served to alienate him from others and vice versa.

Unlike his father, who was often seen throughout the country and in the papers, Emperor Taishō secluded himself from the public. This was also encouraged by military men and politicians looking to take more power for themselves.

Though the movement toward a more Western parliamentary democracy had been growing for some time, it was not until the end of World War I that Japan shifted to a two-party parliamentary system.

Obviously, there were benefits to this since more opinions could be heard and the people had more of a say in government. But this "democratizing" of the country rankled some, especially those with samurai/aristocratic backgrounds. Though the samurai had officially been abolished as a class under Emperor Meiji, old ways, traditions, and ideas were tightly hung onto.

The Japanese emperor still had the final say, but under Taishō, power moved to the *genrō* (men from samurai backgrounds who had supported Emperor Meiji), the Lord Privy Seal, and the head of the Imperial Household.

One of the *genrō*, Saionji Kinmochi, the most powerful politician of the early 1900s, was a believer in expanding parliamentary democracy in Japan. In 1918, a protégé of his, Hara Takashi, became the prime minister. To many on the right, this was a shock. Hara was a commoner, though he did claim some samurai ancestry. Like his mentor, he was liberal and wished Japan to open up more to Western ideas.

Hara also wished to limit the power of the military in Japan. Many of the politicians in the Imperial Diet (Japan's parliament) were in the pockets of the military or simply aligned with them in belief. Among their many beliefs was the idea that Japan needed to expand to survive—and for most, the target of that expansion was China.

Hara also attempted to rein in military spending. It had been increasing exponentially since the start of the 20th century, and by 1920, the deficits were beginning to mount up. Every call for limits on military spending was labeled as a sign of cowardice or a lack of patriotism. Many on the right, in the military, in big business, and in the conservative countryside were also increasingly concerned with the growth of Marxism in Japan, which began to expand in the years after the Bolshevik Revolution in Russia in 1917.

In 1921, Hara was assassinated. The culprit was a right-wing zealot who stabbed him to death while Prime Minister Hara was waiting for a train. This was the start of a series of events that continued into the late 1920s and early 1930s. In the 1920s and 1930s, a series of assassinations and attempted coups took place in Japan. Some of the men killed were local leaders or members of left-wing parties. Others, like Hara, were men of national stature. The culprits were often military men acting without orders as members of secret societies.

In 1932, a group of naval and army cadets assassinated Prime Minister Inukai Tsuyoshi. They received a fifteen-year sentence but were regarded as heroes by many in the nation, which by this time was increasingly under the control and influence of the military and its allies.

As we shall see in the following chapter, a group of Japanese officers in China took it upon themselves to stage an "incident" that would allow them to attack the semi-autonomous Chinese province of Manchuria. Tsuyoshi and his allies in the Imperial Diet (Japan's parliament) were opposed to this annexation, which took place without orders from the military's high command, but it was approved by it after the fact.

In 1936, when the conflict in China expanded further, which many liberal politicians and others protested, groups of Japanese officers and cadets, without orders, went on a killing rampage, killing some former and current officials and causing others to flee. Though these men were caught and executed for going too far, many in the country now feared the military and kept their mouths shut as the military led them into war with China and much of the world.

We will go into more detail on this in the following chapters, but one last point remains. Though Japan's operations in China were meant to increase its empire, power, and prestige around the world, there was another factor: resources.

Manchuria was resource-rich, as opposed to Japan. There was a tremendous amount of coal, some sizable oil fields, and plenty of iron, nickel, and other important commodities. But there was not a lot of good land and food, which Japan's growing population needed. This was one reason for the move into China and other places in Asia in 1940, such as Indochina (which is how Vietnam, Laos, and Cambodia were once known). The problem was that the more Japan expanded, the more resources it needed to protect the resources it had gained, and the one resource it was not able to seize in decent quantities was oil. For that, it was dependent on oil from the Dutch East Indies (today's Indonesia) and, more importantly, the United States, which was, at that time, the largest oil producer and exporter on the planet.

By 1940, Japan's actions in China and Indochina had led it into direct political and economic conflict with the United States, which unilaterally decided to cease the export of oil and steel to Japan. At that point, Japan decided on military action against America.

But that is another story for another time. For now, let us focus on the move of Japan into Manchuria.

Chapter 3 –
Manchuria/Manchukuo

Historians, politicians, diplomats, and journalists, among others, still debate whether or not Japan's invasion of Manchuria in 1931 was the beginning of the Second Sino-Japanese War. To the Chinese, the answer is clearly "yes": Manchuria, historically, was a part of China, Japan invaded it, and they continued on a path of diplomatic harassment, economic warfare, and outright hostility until it invaded China proper (which, as a note, is a term that is only used in the West).

Opinions in Japan differ, though; it really depends on whom you speak to. Some believe that the outbreak of hostilities in Manchuria was the product of rogue army elements acting in concert with Japanese business interests in the area. There is some truth to that assertion. These people often argue that certain "peaceful" elements within Japan attempted to rein in the aggressive wing of the military that ended up going along with the

Manchurian invasion. Others, mainly on the right-wing of modern Japanese politics, see the Manchurian invasion just as it was announced by those who carried it out: a mission to protect Japanese business interests and resources against threatening Chinese mobs and/or warlords. Still others, on the left, see the Japanese invasion of Manchuria as a power grab and the beginning of a well-thought-out plan to invade China and secure its resources for Japan's drive for a bigger empire.

Today, and at the time, most nations of the world saw the Japanese invasion of Manchuria for exactly what it was: a power grab by the ultra-right-wing army officers and an outright power grab by Japan on the Asian mainland. Though it took decades for post-war Japanese governments and many of its people to admit, they have eventually come to the same conclusion.

Okay, so we now have a picture of what people think about the events of 1931. But what actually happened?

First, one might wonder why Manchuria was considered to be a part of China but yet also separate. To understand that, we need to briefly explore the Qing dynasty, the last dynasty of China, which ended in 1912.

The Qing dynasty, sometimes called the "Manchu Dynasty," originated in the area of Manchuria. They were different ethnically from the majority of Chinese, who were known as the Han, and were closer in many ways to their cousins and neighbors, the Mongolians. The initial Qing armies included Mongols, some Han Chinese from the northern areas, and, of course, Manchurians. It is a long and complicated story, involving treachery, peasant revolts, armies, and extended warfare that may have killed more than twenty million people, but in 1644, the Qing declared their dynasty in the north of China and by 1683 had conquered all of China.

The Qing desired to keep Manchuria and attempted for many decades to keep others from settling in the expansive and resource-rich area. The Han Chinese and others were only permitted to settle there under certain rules, but as time went by, hard times in China (including floods, famines, earthquake, and epidemics) forced many Han Chinese and some members of other Chinese ethnic groups to settle in Manchuria. Mongolian and Manchurian landowners were more than happy to let these settlers in to work their lands, as Manchuria was not only underpopulated but exceedingly hard to live in—its extremes in weather are notorious.

By the early 20th century, not only had many non-Manchurian Chinese settled in the territory, but foreign powers and their businesses had moved in as well, along with immigrants. One of the most cosmopolitan cities in Asia at the time was the city of Harbin, where there was not only a sizable Chinese/Manchurian population but also a large number of Koreans and also a large Russian population. It was also filled with Jewish refugees from Tsarist-era pogroms, and, after 1917, Russians fleeing the Bolshevik Revolution and others working to build the Chinese Eastern Railway. Additionally, many Europeans, chasing riches in coal and steel, also settled in Harbin. Even into the mid-1960s, before the official falling-out between the Soviet Union and Communist China, many Russians called Harbin home. Today, a large number of Russian businesspeople live in Harbin, one of China's most populous cities.

The growth of European and Japanese economic, political, and military imperialism in China was not limited to the coastal cities of China, such as Shanghai, Tianjin, Fuzhou, Hong Kong, and its capital, Beijing. After the First Sino-Japanese War of 1896, the Qing granted sizable concessions to Japan in Manchuria. In short order, the Japanese began building railroads within the massive territory (which they claimed was done to improve the area for all living there, which was true to an extent), as well as factories and port facilities.

By the time of Sun Yat-sen's Nationalist revolution and the overthrow of the Qing in 1912, Japan's investments in Manchuria ran into what would be billions of dollars in today's US currency.

The Nationalists had many goals. First and foremost was uniting the country under one regime. As we saw earlier, this was made problematic by the rise of the Communists and the many warlords who controlled wide swathes of the country. As if that were not enough, much of China's resources and its most important cities were controlled, to some degree, by foreigners.

One thing uniting virtually all the Chinese at the time, and at least since the First Opium War of the early 1800s, was the removal of foreign influence. Even the warlords, many of whom made tons of money taking bribes from foreign powers and businesses, still wanted the outsiders out. Of course, questions of power and political differences kept the Chinese at each other's throats while the foreigners continued to make a profit.

This was especially so in Manchuria, where the Japanese *zaibatsu* (a word that roughly translates to a cross between an old-fashioned American trust and a monopoly) wielded great power. Behind the scenes, the Japanese business magnates in Manchuria almost ran the country, along with the military detachments sent there to protect their assets.

Japan and other nations had a great interest in Manchuria, specifically for its coal, iron, and salt, as well as certain crops, which included soybeans, a staple of the Japanese diet. For Japan, which, beginning in the late 1920s and early 1930s, had increased its defense budget many times over and was building perhaps the most modern navy in the world at the time, the resources of Manchuria became a necessity.

From time to time, however, a number of factors interfered with the smooth running of Japanese businesses and the railroads they relied upon in Manchuria. Warlords in remote areas wanted more "taxes" (more like bribes) to allow trains through their territories. Labor unrests sometimes occurred as well, which was usually put down brutally by both the Japanese troops and those of the local warlord.

By the late 1920s, there was no real doubt as to who controlled Manchuria. In 1928, the local warlord Zhang Zuolin was assassinated by troops of the Japanese Kwantung Army, a group of the Imperial Japanese Army that had been ordered to protect Japanese interests in the area. Zuolin had been killed because he attempted to isolate and deprive Japanese concessions in Manchuria of the resources they needed to function. His son, Zhang Xueliang, eventually commanded a private army of 200,000 men, with which he, for a time, supported Chiang Kai-shek, who, as mentioned before, was one of Sun Yat-sen's close allies, when the Japanese invaded China itself.

Japan was not the only nation with sizable interests in Manchuria. The Soviet Union had extensive lumber interests, among others, in the eastern part of the territory, and they, too, experienced some of the same difficulties as the Japanese. In 1928, Zhang Xueliang and the Soviet Union actually went to war over control of the Chinese Eastern Railroad, which brought resources from China and Manchuria to the Soviet Union. This large-scale conflict alarmed the Japanese, who wanted to avoid any interruption in their supplies, but it also showed them the weaknesses of the Chinese and warlord forces in the area. Additionally, the assertion of control by the Soviets in the western part of the territory alarmed the Japanese, who saw the possibility of eventual Soviet movement into their zone of control, which would not only threaten their economic interests but also bring communism that much closer to Japan itself.

Within the Japanese Kwantung Army, like the Imperial Japanese Army at home, there were political cliques and divisions. It is safe to say that by 1931, the officer corps, and likely the men in the lower ranks as well, had come to the conclusion that Manchuria ought to be absorbed into the Empire of Japan. Within this group, some granted that Manchuria should be a part of Japan's sphere of influence but would never consider acting against or without orders. Others, though, were willing to take the extra step. To these men, many of the politicians in Tokyo were cowardly "democrats" without a drop of true Japanese blood in them, i.e., they lacked the "samurai spirit." To these young men, it was not only cowardly politicians but also old and out of touch generals who were too timid to act themselves.

In the fall and winter of 1930 and into the early spring of 1931, younger officers within the Kwantung began agitating for action to take over the entire territory. In addition to insubordinate behavior, they plotted in what they thought was secret and attempted to force the Chinese and warlord forces, as well as the general public, into taking action against Japanese interests.

In Tokyo, senior officers, as well as politicians who believed the time was not right for war, were talking of going to Manchuria to dismiss and/or punish disobedient officers and men. However, word got to the conspirators, and they decided to put into motion plans they had been working on since the winter.

So, it was by the late spring of 1931 that a cabal of officers in the Kwantung Army, led by Colonels Seishirō Itagaki and Kenji Doihara, Lieutenant Colonel Kanji Ishiwara, and Major Takayoshi Tanaka (in this case, the major's family name is second as in the Western style), perfected their plan. They just had to wait for the right time to act.

That time came on September 18th, 1931. A young lieutenant, whose unit guarded a section of the South Manchuria Railway, placed a very weak explosive charge near the tracks. The charge was actually mostly "gun cotton," an unstable and weak explosive sometimes used in minor mining operations. When the charge went off at around 10:20 p.m., the railway was barely damaged, and a Chinese train passed over it shortly thereafter. Still, the conspirators roused their men and prepared to attack the closest Chinese military garrison in response to the "naked aggression" of the Chinese. Later that day, Japanese photographers and supposed experts were hustled out to the site to take pictures of the "Chinese sabotage." As you can see from the picture on the next page, what damage there was was minor indeed. I think it goes without saying that these experts claimed that what they were looking at was not minor at all, as it was damage wrought by "Chinese terrorists" who interfered with the smooth operation of Japanese businesses and military interests.

The damage, barely visible, is circled.
https://commons.wikimedia.org/wiki/File:193109_mukden_incident_railway_sabotage.jpg

On the morning of September 19th, the Japanese army unit at nearby Mukden opened fire on the local Chinese garrison. The few planes of warlord Zhang Xueliang's air force were wrecked, and 500 Japanese soldiers, many of whom had years of pent-up hostility toward the Chinese to release, came screaming into the Chinese garrison.

The Chinese army base contained around 7,000 men, outmatching the Japanese force fourteen to one. However, the Japanese troops were well-trained, disciplined, and well-armed. The Chinese troops facing them were exactly the opposite. Most troops in the warlords' armies, except for special units and personal guards (who were paid much more and given more privileges), were poorly trained peasants, who had joined to feed themselves and perhaps make a little extra money to feed their families. It was not unheard of for men to move between a warlord's army if they heard one was paying more than another. Loyalty was virtually nonexistent, field discipline and motivation were poor, and some did not even possess firearms. By the evening of September 19th, the fighting was over. Two Japanese soldiers had died, while 500 Chinese lost their lives.

At the main headquarters of the Japanese Kwantung Army, Commanding General Shigeru Honjō was shocked that officers under his command had acted without orders. He had known of the plan but ordered the men to wait until further notice. In a combination of being hasty and the time-honored tradition of believing they were acting according to the deepest but unspoken wishes of their commander, the cabal of officers listed above had moved without authority. Their argument to their commander also likely included the idea that if their attack had failed, the general could plausibly deny knowledge of the operation and punish those who failed for disobeying orders.

Lieutenant Colonel Ishiwara expected that he would be dishonorably discharged, at the very least, for disobeying orders, but he hoped that the actions of his group would propel events beyond their control. He argued to General Honjō that the time was right for the invasion of Manchuria or, at the very least, the seizure of the entire city of Mukden (which was already mostly done). After some argument, Honjō agreed and communicated with the commander of the Japanese forces in Korea, another ultra-militarist general, for reinforcements, which were sent.

After the initial assault on the Chinese barracks of Zhang Xueliang, the Japanese moved out to take control of the other cities in Manchuria, beginning with the cities of Changchun and Antung and then eventually the whole nation, including the rich province of Heilongjiang, home to the city of Harbin.

Zhang Xueliang ordered his men to hide their weapons and wait to fight another day. He then began to seek out coordination and communication with Chiang Kai-shek, an enemy of his father. Official Chinese units in Harbin and other important areas were ordered by their generals to put up a fight, but within five months, the entire territory was in Japanese hands.

The Japanese took a number of steps to try to legitimize their seizure of Manchuria in the eyes of the world. For one, they declared the former Qing emperor, Puyi, now 23, the emperor of the new state of Manchukuo in the vain hope that the royalists in China, especially among the warlords, might rally to him. They issued currency, a flag, formed a rump parliament, and set up the capital in Hsinking (then known as Changchun).

All of these things fooled no one except those wanting to be fooled, such as Puyi, though even he got the drift when he almost immediately began having to follow the orders of the Japanese generals in charge.

The Japanese seizure of Manchuria was the biggest international crisis faced by the League of Nations, the international body set up after World War I to attempt to ensure peace in the world. In its biggest challenge since it had been founded, the League failed miserably. In response to the Japanese invasion, the League formed the Lytton Commission, with

British Lord Victory Bulwer-Lytton in charge. Sometime later, the five-member commission agreed that Japan had violated the basic tenets of the League of Nations and was the aggressor against China, which was recognized as the de facto ruler of Manchuria. The Lytton Report announced that Japan's invasion and the state of Manchukuo should not be recognized by any country and that Japan should remove its troops from the area. Additionally, China should be formally recognized as having control over Manchuria.

Of course, this did not please the Japanese at all, and in response (and very dramatically), their representative to the League of Nations read a short speech to its members, which announced Japan's departure from the League, and then marched out of the hall. This happened almost two years after Japan's operations to seize the territory.

This left the members of the League of Nations with a choice. The main purpose of the League was to prevent aggressive warfare. Now, faced with one and clearly having taken a position on it, the League had to decide. Well, it could not decide, and in the end, it did nothing.

Those on the sidelines, such as the fascist dictator of Italy, Benito Mussolini, took notice. The future dictator of Germany, Adolf Hitler, who was on the cusp of power in 1932, did as well. Italy's invasion of Ethiopia in 1936 and Hitler's remilitarization of the Rhineland, which were both in violation of the League's policies, were a direct result of the organization's paralysis over Manchukuo.

The United States, whose actions in response to Japan's aggression in China and elsewhere would later bring it into direct conflict with the island nation, announced the Stimson Doctrine (after US Secretary of State Henry L. Stimson), in which it vowed not to recognize any further Japanese aggression, whether it was in China or somewhere else.

Looking back with 20/20 hindsight, the invasion of Manchuria doomed Japan. At the end of World War II, which, in truth, began in 1931, Japan's major cities were virtually flattened. Millions of its citizens had been killed in the American bombings. It was reduced to bringing in supplies from the territories it still held in wooden junks (a type of Asian sailing vessel) because US submarines controlled its waters and sank everything that moved.

This was all started by Japan's success in Manchuria, which, along with the invasion of China that followed a few years later, put the Japanese military and its fascist ideology in power. Civilian power in Japan, such as it was, declined rapidly after the success of the Japanese invasion of Manchuria. From that point on, the only true debate within Japan took place between the Imperial Japanese Army and Navy, who debated with each other about which way was best to take over the rest of Asia.

Chapter 4 – China Proper

"Do not start a land war in Asia." While this quote may be most famously recognized as coming from the cult classic movie The Princess Bride (1987), it existed before that, but no one is actually sure who first uttered it. It may have been Douglas MacArthur, Dwight D. Eisenhower, or British Field Marshal Bernard Montgomery, or maybe it was someone else entirely. Either way, it makes sense, and the Japanese should have at least paid attention to the idea, though their invasion of China came 51 years before the movie. It was in 1936 that those in power in Japan decided that they might as well attack China too.

What led them to that decision? There are many. For a group of men driven by a philosophy that extolled martial conduct and war, it was only natural. Second, China was a huge, rich, and divided nation. Besides that, given the reaction on the part of the world between 1931 and 1933 to the invasion of Manchuria, it was likely that the European powers and the United States (who were now all in the depths of economic depression and worried about overthrow from within) were likely to do the same thing they had done in 1931—nothing.

From the viewpoint of the Japanese military, the invasion of China made perfect sense.

By the 1930s, Japan was in the grip of what can only be described as fascism. Some have even described the Japanese attitude as an Asian form of National Socialism, which is commonly referred to as Nazism, because within the militaristic beliefs of the ruling officer class, there was a not so subtle belief that the Japanese, as a race, were superior.

Hadn't their history shown this? The islands had never been successfully invaded. As a matter of fact, it was clear to anyone in Japan that the gods had protected Japan by sending the kamikaze, or "divine winds" when the Mongols tried to invade in the 13th century. Everything about Japan from the early Middle Ages to the time of the Second Sino-Japanese War had clearly spelled out that Japan was a special place, as it was a country of military superiority. The samurai, a warrior class renowned throughout the world for its prowess in battle, had ruled Japan since that time of the Mongol invasion, and though civilians were ostensibly supposed to be in charge in Japan after the Meiji Restoration, many of them had samurai backgrounds. And from the 1920s onward, the military had only grown in strength.

Within Japan, the military and their allies in heavy industry (who were the beneficiaries of a huge military buildup), held the control. Virtually all of the organs of government were controlled or influenced by the military. Japanese children were thoroughly inculcated in martial thinking; they were taught about the infallibility of the emperor and those who ruled in his name (the military), were told of Japanese superiority in virtually everything, and were indoctrinated in the ways of Bushidō, "the way of the warrior," which was a sort of code of conduct formulated over centuries of samurai rule. It was now used in a perverse way to drive the Japanese population into believing the idea of subservience to their emperor unto death, the insignificance of the individual, and the idea of death in battle as the ultimate sacrifice and honor.

The simplified and brutal Bushidō taught in schools throughout the 1930s barely reflected the ideals of the samurai, which did call for the ultimate suppression of the individual in battle but also called for the cultivation of personal responsibility, the encouragement of individual cultural growth, and even individual responsibility in the face of injustice.

Almost anyone looking at the situation in Japan with clear eyes in the early 1930s could tell you (and plenty of diplomats, soldiers, sailors, and students from the US and elsewhere did so) that Japan was gearing up for war—a big one.

In the United States, there had been a clear affinity for China for quite some time. Though the US had indeed taken part in some of the more imperialistic policies of the West in China, it was widely seen in the US, and by many in China, that the Americans were the best of the lot. In many ways, the people of the United States saw the downtrodden people of China much like they had been in the years before the American Revolution: much of their land controlled by others, with no say in their own lives. Increasing American sympathy for the Chinese only increased as tales of the crushing poverty and unfairness of Chinese peasants' lives were brought back by American missionaries, but perhaps the biggest effect on the American populace was the publication of Pearl S. Buck's classic novel, The Good Earth, which is about the struggles of Chinese peasants to simply live. The book was massively popular in the US and increased the growing popular sympathy in the US for China and its people.

Chapter 5 – Another "Incident"

On July 7th, 1937, the Japanese attacked China at the Marco Polo Bridge near Beijing. In truth, this action, which is widely considered to be the beginning of the Second Sino-Japanese War (and by some historians as the start of World War II), was only the worst of a string of incidents between the Japanese and Chinese forces. Until this point, the Chinese had been wise in not provoking further battles with the Japanese, for they were not at all prepared to take on the might of the Imperial Japanese Army. There were many reasons for this, many of which have already been touched upon, such as their poorly trained troops, corrupt officers, and poor equipment. Chiang Kai-shek, by this time in an unassailable position within the Kuomintang, was trying to improve things—in a strange turn of fate, China had hired a significant number of foreign officers to train their armies and had bought weapons from Europe as well. The vast majority of these officers and most of the equipment actually came from Germany, including Nazi Germany after 1933. Soon, German weapons were killing Japanese troops.

The problem for Chiang was that his decision to not engage the Japanese in a full-scale war was smart from a military point of view; however, from a political point of view, it was not. The Chinese sentiment against the Japanese was strong, and the Communists made great use of Chiang's inaction to win people over to their side, especially in the countryside. Even within his own party, the ruling Kuomintang (also known as the Chinese Nationalist Party), Chiang came under fire for "capitulating" to increasingly burdensome and insulting Japanese demands.

Chiang's relative inaction also frustrated the Japanese military, which at this point was essentially synonymous with the government, as it was looking for any excuse to start a full-scale war with China and take its resources for itself. On July 7th, 1937, they finally were able to push Chiang and China to the point of no return.

In most of China's major eastern cities, foreign powers not only had their concessions but troops to protect their interests and citizens. These varied in size, but over the course of the late 1920s and early 1930s, they had begun to decrease in size due to a number of factors: cost (the Great Depression caused governments to make massive cuts in their spending), a growing sympathy for the Chinese, and a slow but growing view in the West that the imperialism practiced in China was a thing of the past, or at least should be, were at the top of the list. Still, most forces were sizable enough to protect their interests, and in port cities (whether inland river ports or on the coast), many Western countries, particularly the US and Great Britain, had sizable naval forces.

The one exception was Japan. The forces it kept in its concessions in China kept growing. Few in China believed that much time would go by before there would be another "incident" with Japan.

Marco Polo Bridge over the Yongding River. The bridge takes its name from its mention in the logs of Marco Polo and dates from the 12th century, though it has been restored many times throughout history.
Bairuilong, CC BY-SA 3.0 <https://creativecommons.org/licenses/by-sa/3.0>, via Wikimedia Commons https://commons.wikimedia.org/wiki/File:Marco_Polo-bron_sydsida.JPG

After the Boxer Rebellion, which took place between 1900 and 1901, part of the agreement China reached with foreign powers was that they would be allowed to station troops along the railroad between Beijing, which had been the capital of China for centuries until Chiang Kai-shek moved it for strategic and political reasons to Nanjing in 1927, and Tianjin, the closest major coastal port some seventy miles away and the hub for supplies coming into Beijing. Many of these supplies and goods were of foreign origin, but a significant amount of food came into the city via Tianjin, which made the foreigners' demands even more insulting since foreign troops would guard the railway bringing food into arguably the most important city in China or, at least, the most symbolic one.

By the summer of 1937, the Japanese forces in China itself numbered over 20,000. Most of these troops were stationed in bases near railways, many in the Beijing-Tianjin area. This was already way over the limit set by the agreement in 1901, but what the Chinese did not know was that the number of Japanese forces was increasing almost daily, as it was done in secret, and by the start of July, these forces essentially had the ancient Chinese imperial city surrounded.

On the night of July 7th, Japanese forces were ostensibly conducting military exercises near their base on the outskirts of Beijing at Fengtai and near the ancient Wanping Fortress, to which the Marco Polo Bridge led. At some point, near 11 p.m., Japanese and Chinese troops began to fire on each other. To this day, no one is truly sure what exactly transpired that night. When things calmed down an hour or so later, it turned out that a Japanese private had failed to return to his post.

The Japanese commander sent a message to the Chinese, demanding that his troops be allowed to search for their missing man. Part of the demand involved searching the ancient fortress of Wanping. All of the events of the past few hours, in combination with the latest Japanese demands to search an important historic site, were all insults not only to Chinese honor but also to established international norms and Chinese national pride. Thus, the Chinese commander refused. Hours later, the Japanese soldier, a private named Shimura Kikujiro, returned to his unit after likely being lost in the darkness, but it was too late. In his absence, events had spiraled out of control. A Japanese attack on the fortress was turned back sometime between 12:30 a.m. to 1 a.m.

By two in the morning, the local Chinese commander sent the mayor of Wanping to the Japanese to negotiate a truce. The Japanese refused and demanded to be let into the town to determine the cause of the original incident, but this was likely only a ruse to take the city. This demand was refused.

By 4 a.m., both sides had been in contact with other units in the area. By 4:30, Japanese units surrounded the area around the town, but not before the Chinese reinforcements arrived. By five o'clock, the firing had already begun. The key to entering Wanping and then Beijing itself was the Marco Polo Bridge, and it was there that a full-scale battle erupted.

The Chinese were able to hold the bridge but at a high cost to themselves, and anyways, they were likely to be pushed out of their positions in a relatively short period of time. News of the battle had already reached the highest levels of the Japanese government in China, as well as the Chinese military. Negotiations between representatives of the Japanese Foreign Service and the Chinese general in the area resulted in a verbal agreement that called for a number of things, all of them insulting to Chinese national honor. This agreement included issuing an apology to the Japanese and punishing the Chinese troops that the Japanese believed had fired upon them first.

Within the Chinese ranks, there were significant differences of opinion. Some of the units in the area were essentially under Communist control and refused to accept any truce with the Japanese. Some Nationalist troops pulled back, while others did not. Things were chaotic, and to add to the confusion, the Japanese commanders in the area did not think the terms went far enough and cited the continued firing of some Chinese troops as a reason to keep shelling Wanping. This continued on and off through July 9th.

On July 10th, Japanese armored units arrived in the area and joined the attack on Wanping. At this point, there was no choice but for Chiang Kai-shek to announce that the Kuomintang would resist the Japanese with all the forces they could muster. This was the beginning of the Second Sino-Japanese War, which started in the year 1937 and ended in 1945.

Within days, fighting spread throughout China, especially in the Beijing area, where the Japanese were strongest and close to their main base of operations in Manchukuo. By the third week of July, the Japanese had reinforced their positions in the Beijing area, reaching almost 200,000 men. After a long and complicated battle, in which some Chinese armies were given free passage out of the city while others refused to leave, the ancient imperial capital of China fell to the Japanese at the end of the month.

In the first couple of months of the war, the Japanese took two of China's major cities. As you just read, the first was Beijing and its surrounding area and port, Tianjin. The second was far to the south. Today, that city, Shanghai, is the world's most populous, with a staggering 24 million people living within it. In 1937, a rough estimate was about five million, which was still one of the largest on Earth and one of the richest and most cosmopolitan in China. It was also, in many ways, the most international, with troops and delegations from many different European countries represented there. Of course, the Japanese had sizable numbers of troops in the area, meaning they could resupply and reinforce them quickly, especially since Shanghai was a seaport.

In 1932, there had been yet another "incident" between the Japanese and Chinese in Shanghai. This is known as the January 28th Incident and was, like the other events of the time, much more than that word describes. It started after a group of ultra-nationalist Japanese Zen Buddhist monks were attacked by an anti-foreign Chinese mob, which resulted in a month and a half of pitched battles. Although it "luckily" remained localized, the Chinese, yet again, had to make major concessions to the Japanese, but full-scale war was averted.

The January 28th Incident was also famous, or infamous, for something else, something that has managed to be left out of most history books, at least in the West and in Japan. During the battle, the Japanese launched what is likely the first carrier-launched air assault in history. The same attack can claim another dubious title—it was perhaps the first major terror bombing since World War I. In other words, the Japanese began the modern era of bombing a civilian population solely to cow them into submission.

Five years later, with Japan opening a much wider offensive and China, whose patience for Japanese demands were at an end, in a slightly better position militarily, full-scale war broke out in Shanghai. In the years since, many have called it "the forgotten Stalingrad" of the Far East due to the hard and desperate fighting that took place there in 1937. The Battle of Shanghai, which is sometimes overlooked in the West, cost 300,000 lives. That is almost more than the United States lost in the whole of World War II, and it happened only over the course of two and a half months.

For much of the war, the Japanese held the initiative, but in this case, it was Chiang Kai-shek who decided that there should be a battle in Shanghai. This was done for many reasons, including the fact that they could interrupt the Japanese being resupplied by their navy in some manner. Shanghai was also far from Japan's center of operations in Manchuria/Manchukuo, located in northern China, where they had the bulk of their troops. Lastly, Shanghai was home to the most foreigners and foreign concessions in China, and Chiang believed that a Japanese assault there might affect the Western powers and their interests, which would hopefully, at the very least, get them more involved in the conflict. By 1937, most of the West was decidedly anti-Japanese.

The Japanese, at the time the battle occurred, were more focused on consolidating their hold on northern China and then plotting their next moves. They were also keen on keeping an eye on the Soviet Union, which was backing the Chinese Communists with weapons and advisors in their fight against both the Nationalists and the Japanese. In 1939, the Soviets and the Japanese fought a pitched battle at Khalkhin Gol in Mongolia. It was a crushing Japanese defeat and made them very wary of engaging the Soviets again. For the Soviets' part, they were more concerned with the growing threat of Adolf Hitler and were not interested in pursuing a war with Japan, but this is all a story for another time.

The Battle of Shanghai in 1937 involved perhaps one million troops: 700,000 Chinese and 300,000 Japanese. As you read about this battle and the rest of the war, you should keep in mind a couple of things. The first is something which has been mentioned many times already, the Chinese troops, with some notable exceptions, were poorly trained (especially at the start of the conflict) and poorly equipped. Many were also poorly motivated, especially in the ranks of the Nationalist armies, where many had been conscripted, some forcibly. This differed greatly from the Communist forces, where the vast majority were volunteers. Still, sometimes these conscripts fought bravely and, on many occasions, were joined in battle by more experienced, better-led, and better-equipped volunteer and/or elite units.

The Japanese, though outnumbered over two to one, had a few decisive advantages. First, their infantry and marines were better trained, led, and equipped. The Japanese also had a great advantage in planes (500 newer models versus the 200 varied new and outdated planes for the Chinese), and in its naval forces, and it was the Imperial Japanese Navy that actually urged on the battle in Shanghai.

Throughout the war to come, the Imperial Japanese Army and Navy were frequently at odds. There were a number of points of contention, but arguably the two most important were the fact that the army saw the establishment of a land empire in Asia as its goal. Of course, it would—it was a land-fighting force. Unfortunately, many in the army looked at the navy as more of a transport and supply service than as a fighting force.

The Imperial Japanese Navy could rightly claim credit for the bulk of the more important battles fought in Japan's rise to world power. It had defeated China at sea in 1896, without which there might have been no land battles for the army to fight, and though the Imperial Japanese Army did defeat the Russians on land the Russo-Japanese War, which lasted between 1904 and 1905, their battles were not as decisive, glorious, or shocking to the world as the Imperial Japanese Navy's two victories over the Russian Navy.

The Japanese navy was also the repository of much of the military spending of the nation, and in the 1930s and into the early 1940s, the Imperial Japanese Navy was among the most modern in the world, if not *the* most modern. Having a strong power on the seas was seen, not only by Japan but by most nations, as a way to not only project power but also to seize and/or protect far-flung resources and gain national prestige.

In Shanghai, the Imperial Japanese Navy saw not only existing Japanese interests but also a port from which they could control the flow of goods, supplies, and reinforcements into the interior of China and prevent the Chinese from doing the same. So, in the angry atmosphere of China in early August 1937, a Japanese officer attempted to force his way through a Chinese checkpoint guarding a local airport, which was off-limits to the Japanese. As he sped through, he opened fire on the Chinese, who retaliated and killed the Japanese officer.

International delegations attempted to mediate between the two sides, but neither was interested, and the Japanese threatened further action at the same time they began to bring in reinforcements. For their part, the Chinese did the same, bringing in some of their best units—German-trained and well-equipped officers and men from a variety of divisions. Some German officers, who were expressly forbidden from taking part in any battle, did observe and advise Chinese troops in the city.

The Japanese, although they had been reinforcing their troops in Shanghai, were at first vastly outnumbered and driven into their concessionary area in the city, where the Japanese marines fought bitterly to keep a foothold in the city. The fighting was an indication of what the rest of the war was going to be like—no quarter asked or given.

As would happen in Stalingrad a few years later, intense urban combat broke out, which neither side was truly prepared for. The Chinese numbers were negated by the ability of the Japanese to make fortresses out of buildings, streets, and walled areas of the city. The Chinese, knowing that the Japanese were likely to reinforce and go on the offensive if they could not be removed from the city, conducted ill-advised frontal charges against entrenched Japanese positions, which cost them dearly. Not only were the numbers high, but many of those who fell were those motivated German-trained troops that were the pride of Chiang's army. They had taken years to prepare and equip, and many of them were lost in days or weeks.

As the Chinese expected, the Japanese soon counterattacked, backed by tanks and air forces. The Japanese forces are estimated to have had about 300 tanks in the city, while the Chinese could not scrape together 50 armored vehicles. By the end of November 1937, those Chinese, who were able to, retreated and left the city to the Japanese. Any exact totals of casualties in the Battle of Shanghai are difficult to come by, but estimates put the Chinese military losses at somewhere between 100,000 to 150,000 dead and wounded. The Japanese losses were estimated by historians at Osprey Publishing (a military history specialty publisher) at nearly 19,000 dead, with up to 40,000 wounded.

Today in Shanghai, work is being done to restore one of the most important sites of the Battle of Shanghai, the Sihang Warehouse, better known in China as the "800-man warehouse," in which 400 men under the command of Lieutenant Colonel Xie Jinyuan held out against repeated assaults by the numerically superior Japanese troops. The discrepancy in the name and the actual numbers was intentional: Xie let slip that he had 800 men in the warehouse to throw off the Japanese. Their commander died in the fighting, but many of the men survived Japanese captivity and the war. Some left for Taiwan in 1949 when China fell to the Communists, while others remained, most of them persecuted during the Cultural Revolution. Today, the men are considered to be heroes.

At the end of November 1937, the Japanese controlled a vast area of northern China and were now in control of one of its most important ports, located midway down the coast. The next move it would make would be to take Chiang's capital of Nanjing, known in the West at the time as Nanking.

Chapter 6 – The Opponents

Before we speak of the terrible events that occurred in Nanjing, let's look at the opposing forces of the Chinese and Japanese in the war. Much of the information in this chapter comes from two sources: *The Oxford Companion to WWII,* and *The Oxford Companion to Military History.*

In 1937, the Chinese Nationalist forces under the direct command of Chiang Kai-shek numbered near 300,000 men. Of these, 80,000 were considered elite and had been highly trained and equipped with the most modern weapons. These were often referred to as the "Generalissimo's Own," after the title that Chiang took for himself.

In addition to these 300,000 or so men, a further 1.2 million were ostensibly under Chiang's command but were more of a hodge-podge of units with varied levels of training, ability, and equipment. The quality of their leadership varied widely as well. Many of these troops were loyal to local warlords or Kuomintang generals but had varying levels of loyalty to Chiang. By 1939, the Nationalist ranks had swollen to about 2.5 million men, and at the end of the war, Nationalist leaders counted their forces at about 5 million, though this was a padded number, and besides, many of the troops were of both dubious quality, motivation, and loyalty.

In addition to the Nationalist troops, the Japanese faced the troops of the Communist Party of China. The Communist forces were divided along similar lines as the Nationalist forces in that there were essentially two types of forces, "regular" and "irregular." The regular formations of the Communists consisted of, for the most part, two formations, the Eighth Route Army and the New Fourth Army, which operated in northern and central China, respectively. The Communists had only guerrilla and local militia forces in the south of the country. In 1937, these two units numbered just under 100,000 men, which included a sizable number of women as support troops and occasionally in combat. By 1940, the ranks of these units had grown to half a million men, shrinking (through attrition, disease, defection, etc.) to about 450,000, a number they held for most of the war. By the summer of 1945, however, when it was clear to everyone that Japan would soon be beaten and that the Chinese Civil War would flare up once more, the Communist ranks had grown to just under a million people.

Chinese Weaponry and Forces

The weapons supplied to the men in the Nationalist ranks were varied and depended both on access and capture. Before the war, the Nationalist forces, at least those most loyal to Chiang Kai-shek, were equipped with relatively modern German weapons. These did not include tanks, which the Germans were developing and producing for their own use in Hitler's upcoming plans, or planes, which, before Hitler, were forbidden by the Versailles Treaty that ended World War I. After Hitler's ascension, most German planes were kept in Germany for the upcoming conflict as well.

However, the Chinese had abundant supplies of one of the best bolt-action weapons of the war, the Mauser 98k, which they both imported and produced under license. They also imported Mauser-style rifles and carbines made under license in Belgium and Czechoslovakia. Hundreds of thousands of earlier Mauser models, the Gewehr 88, were also sent ("98" and "88" were designations for the year they were first approved for use in the German military).

China imported a variety of machine guns from many different nations as well. This was due to limitations on both supply and shipping, as well as interruptions in supply due to political reasons, both within China and overseas. Russian, Finnish, Swiss, and Czech squad light machine guns were imported, but barrels and other parts became scarce, as did the correct ammunition. The Chinese troops were always at a disadvantage compared to the Japanese when it came to automatic weapons, being outgunned three to one.

Artillery was also problematic. At the beginning of the war, the roughly 800 heavy artillery guns in the Nationalist ranks were kept under Chiang's direct control. The reason behind this was two-fold, but only one of the following reasons held much water. The first was trying to keep the available artillery centralized and not spread out in penny packets (small units), so at least they might be effective in a major battle with the Japanese. The second, and more important reason, at least to Chiang, was that by keeping heavy guns under his direct control, he had leverage over any ambitious and/or disloyal subordinate or warlord. Because of this, great numbers of mortars were imported and made within China.

In later years, the Nationalists did gain artillery, which were sent by Britain and the US, but since the supply routes were so long, this was an unreliable supply. Toward the end of the war, the Communists benefited from their relationship with the Soviet Union, which was never at a loss for artillery. Combined with other factors, the use of heavy Soviet-made artillery helped the Chinese Communists win the Chinese Civil War after the Japanese were defeated.

The Chinese were at a distinct disadvantage in regard to armored vehicles, as they were in many other areas except manpower. Before the war, they had purchased small numbers of British and French light tanks and tankettes (a pre-war designation that describes a cross between a lightly armored truck/jeep and a light tank). During the war, the Soviets did send a number of outdated BA-10 and BA-20 armored cars, as well as T26 light tanks, which, when used properly by trained crews against Japanese tanks, could be effective, but this rarely happened.

The story of the Chinese Nationalist Air Force (or "ROCAF" for "Republic of China Air Force") is an interesting one, which we will touch upon more in another chapter, but at the start of the war, the Chinese were outgunned in this department as well. In 1937, the Chinese had somewhere between 200 to 250 combat aircraft, depending on which source you are looking at.

The airplanes of the Chinese air force were a hodge-podge of planes from other nations. At the start of the conflict, the Chinese air force consisted of monoplane American Boeing P-26 "Peashooter" fighters and Curtiss BF2C-1 Goshawk biplanes. Both were obsolete by the time the war in China began.

The Goshawk was one of the last biplane fighters produced, rolling off the line in 1933. They were designed specifically for export, and only 164 were made. Most of these went to China, though a few went to military dictatorships in Latin America. The plane had a maximum speed of 255 miles per hour (which was truer on the drawing board than in reality), a slow rate of climb, carried a strange combination of .30 and .50 caliber machine guns, one under each wing, and had a 500-pound bomb payload.

For keeping down internal dissent or facing down a warlord, these were great planes. They were not when facing the Japanese.

The Boeing "Peashooter" was an open-cockpit monoplane first produced in 1932. Though originally designed as pursuit fighters for the US Army Air Force (the US Air Force did not come into existence until 1947 as a separate part of the US Armed Forces), the plane was shortly made obsolete by developments in aircraft design, and most were exported. Again, China was the main customer. It had a top speed of 234 miles per hour, a ceiling of 27,000 feet, and carried a variety of weapons: two .30 caliber machine guns, one .50 machine gun/.30 machine gun, and two 100-pound bombs/or five 31-pound anti-personnel bombs. In 1938, a massive dogfight between the Japanese Zeroes (talked about below in the section about Japanese weaponry) and Chinese "Peashooters" was the first recorded aerial battle solely between monoplanes.

Boeing "Peashooter" fighter. This plane went up against the Japanese "Zero." The results were not good.
https://commons.wikimedia.org/wiki/File:Peashooter.arp.750pix.jpg

The one fighter plane that the Chinese began to get in numbers as the war went on was the Soviet Polikarpov I-16 "Ishak" ("Donkey"). A small, highly maneuverable plane with a top speed of 326 miles per hour, the I-16, in the hands of a trained pilot, could be a match for the early Zeroes in some situations. It carried two 7.62mm guns or two 20mm cannons and could be equipped with anti-tank rockets or 1,100 pounds of bombs. Over 10,000 of these planes were built, but of course, most of those remained in the Soviet Union for its fight to the death with Hitler. However, a fairly significant number went to China and was a factor in a number of battles in the Second Sino-Japanese War.

Lastly, and most famously, the Chinese were supplied with American pilots flying the Curtiss P-40 Warhawk beginning in the spring of 1941. These were, of course, the famed Flying Tigers. We will devote more attention to this famous formation in the context of American and foreign aid to China later on.

Regarding naval forces, the Chinese were so outmatched that the word "navy" barely applies. Before the war, the Chinese possessed two relatively modern light cruisers. These were sunk in the Yangtze River in the defense of Nanjing in 1937 but were refloated by the Japanese and absorbed into the Imperial Japanese Navy.

The Chinese also possessed a small number of imported German E-boats, a fast torpedo boat akin to the American PT boat. Most of these were sunk, though a few survived to patrol rivers in areas firmly under Chinese control and to transport Chiang Kai-shek and other important personages when necessary.

The remainder of the Chinese naval forces consisted of slap-dash machines used to transport troops with perhaps a machine gun or two mounted on deck or, in the rarest of cases, a captured Japanese cannon, but this was extraordinarily rare. The rest of the Chinese navy consisted of the traditional sailing junks, which were numerous on the coast and major rivers and were used to some effect for smuggling in weapons, personnel, and supplies.

Lastly, though they lacked tanks in any significant numbers, the Chinese did employ armored trains to both transport and support troops, carry supplies, and were used as mobile artillery. The armored train saw the height of its popularity in World War I and the 1920s, but many still survived and were used in World War II, especially over the great distances of the Soviet Union. Others were used to transport important personages from place to place near or in war zones. Adolf Hitler, Hermann Goering, Joseph Stalin, and Chiang Kai-shek all made use of heavily armored trains for personal use.

The Japanese

The number of Japanese forces in China through the Second Sino-Japanese War fluctuated as the conflict went on, dictated both by Japanese actions and necessity. By 1942, the Japanese were in action in China, the Philippines, Indonesia, Malaysia, New Guinea, Vietnam, Burma, and the myriad islands of the Pacific. At times, their forces reached into the Aleutian Islands and India. Additionally, they kept troops in Manchuria/Manchukuo and Korea to help keep an eye on the Soviet Union.

Looking at a map, you can see that the Japanese area of influence and theaters of war were greater in size and more far-flung than that of Germany. Imagine then how the face of the war might have changed if the Japanese had chosen not to invade China and Southeast Asia and instead concentrated their forces against the US in the Pacific or the British Empire in Australia and New Zealand. Of course, the Japanese decision to go to war in China and Southeast Asia led to the American decision to impose an embargo on war-making resources like steel, oil, and coal to Japan, which helped lead to the Japanese decision to attack Pearl Harbor. Still, there were those in Japan that pushed for war against the US for control of the Pacific long before the embargo.

Consider for a moment that the Japanese, at the height of their strength in China, had over a million men in uniform. Some put the figure closer to two million. That is a million or so men that might have been used in the Pacific Campaign had not the Chinese kept them bogged down. Most experts agree that any war between the Japanese and the United States would have ultimately ended in an American victory—the power of American industry, its technological advantages as the war went on, its advantage in manpower, and its virtually endless resources would have ensured it. However, the Americans knew how much bloodier and more prolonged any war with Japan would be without the involvement of the Chinese, which is why, as we will see, the Americans did their best to keep the Chinese well-armed and well-supplied during the war.

But we digress. The Japanese began the war with just over half a million men in China. Most of these were stationed in the newly annexed area of Manchukuo, but a substantial number were based in and around the Japanese concessionary areas, like Beijing. From this number, it is easy to decipher the intent of Japan before the Marco Polo Bridge Incident. Half a million troops were not needed to protect the concessionary areas, and the Soviet Union had shown no intention of becoming involved in Manchukuo, though the Japanese believed they were. The half-million troops were actually there waiting for the opportunity to invade China, regardless of any future Chinese "aggression," which all of the world knew was a ridiculous claim.

By 1939, the Japanese had over a million men in China. These were joined by a small number of Chinese collaborators and a sizable militia in Manchukuo, which was mostly used for keeping order and protecting vital installations and resources. These few hundred thousand men essentially waved the white flag the minute the Soviet and Chinese Communist troops attacked at the very end of the war.

The Japanese troops, however, were (at least at the start of the war) highly motivated and trained. They were well-equipped and generally well-led. These advantages allowed the Japanese to carry the attack to the Chinese and carry the day in most of the pitched battles between the two. However, the image that many in the West have about the one-sided nature of the war in China and the major battles within it is essentially unfounded. While in most of the largest battles of the war, the Japanese prevailed, many of these battles were costly, hard-fought struggles that continually frustrated the Japanese in their search for the decisive battle that would ensure their victory in China.

Japanese Weaponry and Forces

As we have seen, the Japanese enjoyed superiority in every war-fighting category—armored tanks, planes, and ships.

While the Japanese found themselves massively outclassed in regard to tanks when they fought the Soviets in the battle of Khalkhin Gol in 1939 and against the Americans in the Pacific, their superiority in tanks in China helped them to not only win battles but to also keep the population in line in areas under their control.

Although the Japanese developed a series of heavier medium tanks during the war, most of these never saw action and were planned to be used during the expected American invasion of Japan. One, the Type 97, did see action in the Philippines and one or two other places during the war. However, while it was the best Japanese medium tank of the war years, it was still outclassed by even the worst American and British tanks put into the field. One heavy or super-heavy tank was designed by the Japanese, but it was so impractical that it was never put into development. For the duration of the war, both in China and in other theaters of the conflict, the Japanese relied on a series of light and medium tanks, Types

89, 95, and 98.

The Type 89 "I-Go" ("I-Go" refers to it being the first model, which is sometimes written as "Chi-Ro") weighed 12.8 tons, was 5.73 meters long, 2.56 meters high, and 2.15 meters wide. It carried a crew of four within its riveted armor and was armed with a 57mm gun and 100 rounds. Its anti-infantry weapons were two 6.5mm machine guns (one forward-facing in the hull, the other in the rear of the turret). It could reach a top speed of 16 miles per hour. For its weight, the tank was well-armed but was also extremely under-powered and under-armored, as it was just 17mm at its thickest.

The Type 89 had been designed in 1928 and went out of production in 1942, as it was replaced by the Type 98. The Type 89 was the main tank deployed by the Japanese in the Battle of Khalkhin Gol with the Soviets, and it was thoroughly outclassed by even the most obsolete Soviet tanks, something that the Soviets took careful note of.

The Type 95, (known as the "Ha-Go" or sometimes the "Ke-Go," both of which refer to it being the third model) which was a replacement for the slower Type 89, also saw action against the Soviets, as well as in Southeast Asia and India against the British. This tank also saw action in the Philippines and the Pacific against the Americans. It has the dubious distinction of being the only hostile armored vehicle to ever enter American soil, which occurred during the Aleutian Islands campaign. Near the end of the war, the Japanese 18th and 14th Tank Divisions engaged the British in southern China, near the border of Burma, and were annihilated by the newly arrived Sherman M3 tanks sent from North Africa. The Type 95, while faster than the Type 89, only carried a 37mm gun and 12mm riveted armor, meaning it improved on speed but virtually nothing else.

One of the main problems with Japanese tank development was that there was only so much steel to go around. At the beginning of this book, we learned that one of the main reasons for the Japanese beginning the Second Sino-Japanese War was its lack of raw materials, which modern nations needed to be able to fight. In the case of steel, the Imperial Japanese Navy had priority. The navy's argument was logical: on an island nation, its first line of defense was its navy. Following that, Japan could only expand overseas, and the navy was the only method of transportation and protection. Once the Empire of Japan was established, the defeat of the Allied navies became paramount, for if the Imperial Japanese Navy was annihilated, then everything else would fall apart. Indeed, this is almost exactly what happened in the end. Since the Imperial Japanese Navy had priority, this meant the land forces would receive both a far lesser amount than the navy did and poorer quality materials, which resulted in smaller and poor-quality tanks for the army. This did not matter that much at the beginning of the war since the only opponents they met on land were the Chinese, for the most part. Once the Japanese met Soviet, American, and British tanks, they realized just how inferior their own tanks were, and by that time, the resource situation had only gotten worse for the Japanese, not better. Making more light tanks seemed to be the only answer. It was the wrong one, but the Japanese, in regard to tank production, were between a rock and a hard place.

This also meant that unlike the Allies and Germany's later model tanks, the Japanese continued to produce tanks made from riveted armor. Riveted armor is weaker than welded and cast armor, and the rivets themselves turn into anti-personnel weapons when hit with enough force. The later medium tanks mentioned earlier did use a combination of riveted and cast/welded armor, but again, these tanks were held in Japan for use against the expected American invasion.

So, this meant that the most "modern" Japanese tank in China, the Type 98 (designated "Ke-Ni," meaning "Light Tank 2"), which was developed in 1938, had thicker armor and a more effective two-man turret. However, it still carried the same 37mm gun, which was useless against any real armor. Some variants carried a 20mm gun, but the same held true: it was good against people and wood buildings but bad against armor. Only a couple hundred of these tanks were produced.

Type 98 Ke-Ni, Imperial Japanese Army photo
https://commons.wikimedia.org/wiki/File:Type_98A_Ke-Ni.jpg

Though it did not really affect the war in China (at least not until the end of the war when the Japanese met the British forces in the south and the Soviet forces in the north after the dropping of the atomic bombs), another byproduct of the lack of any real opposition in China was that the Japanese did not learn the lessons of modern tank warfare that everyone else did during the war. Of course, by the time they met the British and Soviets, the war was essentially over for the Japanese anyway.

Naval Forces

The Japanese enjoyed such a superiority over the Chinese in this regard that it really does not require much discussion. Only those with a deep abiding interest in Japanese naval forces in World War II would have an interest in the exact types, specifications, and numbers of ships the Japanese employed in the Chinese theater of the war. Suffice it to say that the Imperial Japanese Navy employed a small number of older battleships, as the more modern ones went to face the Americans after Pearl Harbor, cruisers, destroyers, minesweepers, coastal and riverine gunboats, and a number of submarines to patrol the coast and possibly intercept supplies coming from overseas.

The river systems of eastern China also allowed the Japanese to sail up them a significant distance. For example, in the first days of the Battle of Nanjing, witnesses saw a flotilla of twenty ships making their way up the Yangtze River toward the city. The Chinese had nothing with which to stop them.

Infantry

The Imperial Japanese Army was well-equipped, especially in comparison to their Chinese counterparts and especially in the beginning and middle of the war. Between 1944 and 1945, larger and larger quantities of American, British, and Soviet weapons and ammunition began to make their way into China, and slowly, the Chinese began to be able to fight their enemies on a somewhat equal footing.

Generally speaking, the Japanese infantry weapons were accurate and long-lasting, though their Nambu pistols were notoriously prone to jamming.

The main infantry weapon of Japanese soldiers and marines during the war was the Arisaka rifle, of which there were a few variants. Some older rifles, like the Type 38, made in 1905 (with a carbine model made in 1911), still saw action, as nearly 3.5 million of the weapons were made. However, the main infantry weapon of the war was the Arisaka Type 99. Three and a half million of these weapons were made, and tens of thousands of variants (cavalry carbines, and snipers) were made as well.

Since the end of the war, images of the warriors from different nations with their weapons have been seared into the collective consciousness. The Germans were associated with the Mauser 98k or the MP-40 submachine gun. The Americans had the Thompson submachine gun or the Garand rifle, the Soviets, the PPSh submachine gun, and the British had the STEN submachine gun or the Lee-Enfield rifle. Images throughout the war showed Japanese soldiers with their long Arisaka rifles that had long bayonets attached, sometimes with the Rising Sun Flag of Japan attached as well.

The Arisaka Type 99 fired a 7.7mm cartridge and had an effective range of about 600m, though longer barreled and scoped sniper variants could reach farther. The weapon weighed just under nine pounds. The Type 99 was a bolt-action rifle, and while most of the major combatants of the war moved on to semi-automatic weapons, the Japanese stayed with the Type 99 until the end of the war.

The use of the Arisaka provides a bit of insight into the psychology of the Japanese in World War II. The weapon was a good one, a very good one. A well-trained soldier might be able to get off thirty rounds in a bit more than a minute. But though the question of resources did play into infantry weapon development as it did with armor, there is another more subtle reason why the Arisaka remained the weapon of Japanese soldiers and why more modern weapons were not developed en masse.

Firstly, in the first years of the war (both the Second Sino-Japanese War and the larger encompassing World War II), the Japanese won virtually every battle they fought, and they fought with the Arisaka. They began not only to associate the Arisaka with victory but developed the unfortunate tendency that many successful armies develop—they believed they were unbeatable. This went hand in hand with the notion that the Japanese were superior to their enemies—superior in endurance, loyalty, and fanaticism, among other things. Just as Hitler began to believe that he and his soldiers could move mountains with willpower alone, so did the Japanese. Why develop new weapons when they were both good enough and merely an appendage of the superior "samurai spirit?"

The Arisaka became associated with victory. In Japanese propaganda, Japanese soldiers were seen as being the modern embodiment of the samurai. And since the samurai carried swords, officers were allowed to as well. Since swords were only allowed to be carried by officers, the extra-long bayonet of the Arisaka became a sort of substitute, the enlisted man's samurai sword, and we all know the power of the samurai sword in Japanese history, psychology, and myth.

The Japanese also supplied their soldiers with German 98k Mausers made under license in the pre-war years, as well as Italian Carcano rifles.

Though the Japanese did make use of a small number of excellent German MP 18 pre-war submachine guns, this was neither a popular weapon nor was it widely deployed. Many military historians, as well as Japanese and Allied soldiers, have cited the lack of submachine guns as a glaring weakness of the Japanese infantryman in World War II, for while the army did field light and medium machine guns, there were also relatively heavy two- or three-man weapons, which reduced mobility.

The Japanese began the Manchurian campaign using the Type 11 machine gun. Almost 30,000 of these weapons were made, and can, in a way, be compared to the American Browning Automatic Rifle ("BAR") in looks and in that it was a one-man weapon. However, it was heavy, needed a bipod, and was relatively unreliable.

In 1937, the Japanese developed the Type 96, a 6.5mm light machine gun, which needed a crew of two, weighed 19 pounds, and had a slow fire rate of 250 rounds per minute for accuracy and 550 for cover. The weapon had an effective range of 600m. An approximate total of 41,000 of these guns was made.

In 1939, the Japanese developed a light/medium machine gun that could fire the same round (7.7mm) as their heaviest machine gun, the Type 92 (mostly used in defense), and also developed the Type 99. This was the most produced of the Japanese machine guns of the war, with approximately 53,000 made. This was a two-man weapon as well, but it could be handled by one man when necessary. It was actually equipped with a bayonet, where one can, again, see the "samurai spirit"; however, it was really impractical, as the gun weighed 25.2 pounds. The Type 99 had a maximum firing rate of 800 rounds per minute but was more effective (like most machine guns) in bursts, equaling about 250 rounds per minute. In the Pacific War, US Marines and soldiers learned to be fearful of this weapon, but fortunately, not many were made. As a comparison, the US produced nearly *three million* .30 and .50 caliber machine guns during the war.

The Japanese also produced a wide variety of artillery and mortars during the war, and their mortarmen were considered some of the best of the war. Once again, however, questions of supply and development plagued the Imperial Japanese Army. In China, they enjoyed a practical superiority in artillery and mortars, but in the Pacific, they were massively outgunned by the Americans and British.

Aircraft

During the Second Sino-Japanese War and World War II, there was no "Japanese Air Force"; instead, the army and navy each had their own air forces, much like the United States. Throughout the conflicts, the Japanese flew a staggering variety of planes: fighters, bombers, dive bombers, torpedo bombers, reconnaissance planes, flying boats of all types, transport planes, etc. Within those categories, for instance, bombers and fighters, there were many different types. These were either advancements on existing aircraft or entirely new models.

Though the Japanese flew around twelve different types of fighter planes and six different types of bombers (three medium types and three dive bombers) in China during the war, they are obviously known for one model of their fighter aircraft, the iconic "Zero," officially known as the Mitsubishi A6M "Reisen." The name "Zero" comes from the last digit of the imperial year in which it entered service, Year 2600, or 1940.

The most famous attribute of the Zero was its maneuverability. Simply put, until about late 1942/43, the Zero was the most maneuverable plane in Asia. In the hands of an experienced pilot, the Zero could almost turn on a proverbial dime. And when the Zero was deployed in 1940, it was also one of the fastest production aircraft, topping out at about 330 miles per hour.

The weaknesses of the Zero were partly why the plane was so maneuverable. It was light because it was made primarily of wood. As American pilots gained experience and better aircraft, they learned to fight with the Zero, which they came to regard as a "paper kite," as it would blow apart when hit with a good burst of the .50 caliber machine guns they carried. Still, between 1940 and 1943, the Zero ruled the skies, especially over China, where it was never really challenged except for a short time before the US entered the war. Before the deployment of the Zero, the Imperial Japanese Navy deployed the Mitsubishi A5M "Claude," an open-cockpit monoplane that was the Chinese air force's foe in that first monoplane-only dogfight mentioned earlier.

The Imperial Japanese Army deployed two main fighters in China, the Nakajima Ki-37 "Nate" (its Allied designation) and the improved version, the Nakajima Ki-43 "Hayabusa" (meaning "Peregrine Falcon"), which was called "Oscar" by the Allies.

Although these were manufactured by the Nakajima Corporation rather than the Mitsubishi Corporation (like the Zero), the Nate and the Oscar looked much like the Zero. The Nate was put into the field in 1937 and was the mainstay of the Imperial Japanese Army air forces until 1943, which was when the excellent "Oscar" was deployed in numbers. For all intents and purposes, the Oscar replicated the performance of the Zero, in both its strengths and weaknesses, including a lack of self-sealing gas tanks, which led to many fiery deaths.

Zero
https://commons.wikimedia.org/wiki/File:Captured_A6M5_in_flight_1944.jpeg

Oscar
https://commons.wikimedia.org/wiki/File:Nakajima_Ki-43-IIa.jpg

In its war against China, which included the widespread targeting of civilian targets, the Japanese mainly used the Mitsubishi G4M "Betty" medium bomber. Fortunately for its adversaries, especially in the Pacific, the Betty was built for speed and range, meaning it was light. In turn, this meant that, like the Zero, it had virtually no armor, no self-sealing fuel tanks, and much of the plane's construction was wood. Because of this, the Betty was relatively easy to shoot down.

However, in China, where the Chinese lacked sufficient numbers of anti-aircraft guns, fighter planes, and pilots, and where the Japanese had more than enough escort fighters (for the early part of the conflict at any rate), the Betty and other bombers rained destruction on Chinese cities.

The Betty had a 1,772-mile range, enabling it to be based far enough from enemy armies and most aircraft, for example, in Manchuria and Taiwan (the Japanese had claimed in the First Sino-Japanese War and called Formosa). The Betty carried four 7.7mm machine guns (later models added a 20mm cannon in the tail) and had a payload of about 2,000 pounds in differing mission-dependent configurations. During the war, almost 2,500 Bettys were made. Most of them were deployed to China.

Chapter 7 – The Tragedy of Nanjing

Though the Japanese invasion of Manchuria in 1931 had caused international outrage and a vote against Japan in the League of Nations, not to mention the invasion of China itself following the Marco Polo Bridge Incident that likewise brought international condemnation to Japan, it was not until the Battle of Nanjing and its almost unprecedented violence that the world began to understand the scope of Japan's plans in China and what it was willing to do to carry them out.

In 1940 (three years after the Nanjing Massacre), in a frustrated reaction to the Chinese Communist guerrilla offensive known as the Hundred Regiments Offensive, the Japanese military instituted what became known as the Three Alls Policy strategy. The "Three Alls" was "kill all, burn all, loot all." Officially, it had a more official-sounding, but no less brutal, name, "The Burn to Ash Strategy." Historians have made the argument that the institution of this policy really amounted to a campaign of genocide in China, but long before this policy had a name, the Japanese had begun to kill all, burn all, and loot all in Nanjing, also known as Nanking.

Before the Battle of Shanghai, there had been some within the Japanese military and government that believed that the campaign in China should be halted, if not for good then for a large chunk of time while the army reorganized, refitted, and resupplied. These people also believed that, contrary to their rhetoric, the Chinese would sue for peace. They further argued that Japan controlled a sizable portion of China (larger than Japan itself) and should consolidate its rule and economic gains.

These moderates within the Japanese camp lost out to the militants, and why shouldn't they? The Imperial Japanese Army had been victorious everywhere it fought, and the Chinese were in disarray; though the Nationalists and the Communists had agreed to put aside their differences to fight their common enemy, there were significant differences between the two parties, not only in their political outlook but also in the way they viewed the war against the Japanese and the strategy needed to fight them. On top of that, it was not unheard of for units of the Nationalists and Communists to engage in battle with each other from time to time.

Some Nationalists even wondered whether Chiang Kai-shek was more interested in fighting the Communists than the Japanese. Back in 1936, before the Marco Polo Bridge Incident, but at a time of frequent skirmishes and tension with the Japanese, Chiang had seemed more willing and eager to go after Communist Mao Zedong and his followers than the foreign invaders. Two of the more powerful warlords needed by Chiang actually kidnapped him and publicly extorted a pledge from him to concentrate on the Japanese and make peace with the Communists, at least temporarily.

As we have seen, after the Marco Polo Bridge Incident and the bloody Battle of Shanghai, Chiang announced his party's complete resistance against the Japanese. The Japanese militants pointed to this and their winning campaigns to urge for the further annexation of Chinese territory.

Their next target was Nanjing, which you can see from the map above is located away from the coast, but it was an important port and staging area for goods and transport into the interior of China. Today, the population of Nanjing is over eight million people, which is as much as New York City. In 1937, Nanjing was not a small city either—its population was over one million people, though, by the time of the Japanese siege, many of those who could leave did. These were, for the most part, upper-class Chinese and many (but not all) of the foreigners living in the city. Still, at the time the Japanese began their attack, there were still hundreds of thousands of civilians and soldiers in the city.

Those people today who are aware of the Second Sino-Japanese War and the terrible events of Nanjing sometimes point out the many different population estimates put out before, during, and after the war, as well as the differing totals of the dead when the battle and atrocities ended. Those on the Japanese right-wing use the different numbers to disparage the idea that there was a massacre in Nanjing at all, saying that "Yes, people die in war, but there were no 'massacres.' This is all Chinese and Chinese Communist propaganda."

Iris Chang, in her book *The Rape of Nanking*, placed the total deaths due to the Nanjing Massacre at an estimated 400,000 to 500,000. Australian journalist Harold Timperley, who worked in China before, during, and after the war, put the total at 400,000. The Chinese government generally agrees with these figures. Official Japanese government figures are hard to come by, and to be fair, the current estimates for this massacre is so wide-ranging that no number most likely will never be agreed on, as the current agreement on the death total of the massacre range from 40,000 to 200,000. Japanese right-wing nationalists have put forth numbers as low as only about 10,000 died.

Likely, even if there were exact totals, the fanatic right-wing would still deny any atrocities, but the numbers are problematic. That is easy to understand for the number of reasons cited below.

In the China of 1937 (and actually well into the 1990s), there was virtually no Chinese middle class. People were either at the very top or the very bottom, and when we say bottom, one has to realize that China was a desperately poor country.

This meant that there was no money to go to bureaucracies dedicated to keeping an exact track of the population, and even if there were, China is so massive, and the population at the time was in constant movement, making an exact count nearly impossible.

Add to that, from 1900 (the time of the Boxer Rebellion) to the 1930s, China consistently experienced wars or violent upheavals of some kind or another. Making things worse were amazingly common natural disasters, like floods, famines, and earthquakes, all making census-taking nearly impossible.

Lastly, the war itself destroyed many of the records that did exist. Then, of course, came the end of the Chinese Civil War and the many upheavals of Chinese Communist rule under Mao Zedong (such as the Great Leap Forward of the 1950s to 1960s and the Cultural Revolution of the 1960s to 1970s) when ideas, numbers, records, and many other sources of information were destroyed or distorted. Still, through existing records, contemporaneous accounts, and painstaking work by historians and others, we have a good enough idea of the population of Nanjing at the time.

Some will say, "Why don't we at least have an exact count of the dead?" As macabre as this sounds, Nanjing was not Auschwitz, with its terrifying recordkeeping, and the events of Nanjing were not planned; they were, for the most part, an orgy of violence that was encouraged on the scene outside of the sanctioning of the Japanese government, which tacitly approved of it.

In Nanjing, no Chinese ventured outside when they did not have to, and they certainly did not stop to count bodies in mass graves and piles around the city and its environs. The Japanese did not care at all to record numbers.

The battle and the tragedy that followed officially began on December 13th, 1937. The Japanese, fresh from their victory in Shanghai, moved to capture Chiang's capital quickly and arrived at the gates of Nanjing, just under 200 miles away, in a few days, pushing aside limited Chinese resistance.

The Chinese, having fought hard for Shanghai and still coordinating a defense plan after Chiang's announcement of total war against Japan, were demoralized and disorganized, which is exactly why the Japanese acted so quickly.

The Battle of Nanjing was less a "battle" than a massacre. The Chinese army, under the command of General Tang Shengzhi (who successfully managed to stay alive under the Communists and become governor of the Hunan province for a short time), collapsed, and those units that could fled the city. The panic in trying to flee Nanjing was so intense that some Chinese units fired on one another to get them "out of the way" in their haste to retreat. However, by the time the official order to retreat came, most of the men from over two divisions of Chinese troops had either already fled or were surrounded, which only took the Japanese two days to do.

What followed next was a horror show that sickened the world, even the men in Berlin. (It should be noted that one of the "saviors" of Nanjing was a German diplomat, John Rabe, who—along with other Europeans whose countries the Japanese did not want to antagonize at that point—set up a "safety zone" in the European quarter of Nanjing, saving thousands.) The killing went on for six long weeks.

Some fifty years later, American historian and writer Iris Chang, in her bestseller, *The Rape of Nanking* (1997), put into words what many in Nanjing and China had known, but which for over fifty years (at the time the book was written), the world had chosen to largely ignore. A few years later, Chang would take her own life, the result of poorly treated depression and having immersed herself in the horror of the Second Sino-Japanese War for over ten years. Though Chang received much criticism following the publication of her bestseller, more of that criticism was leveled at her seeming criticism of the Japanese as a people and not over her grasp of the facts, though those on the fanatic Japanese right-wing said her whole book was a lie.

The following are excerpts from her book.

> *The Japanese not only disemboweled, decapitated, and dismembered victims but performed more excruciating varieties of torture. Throughout the city they nailed prisoners to wooden boards and ran over them with tanks, crucified them to trees and electrical posts, carved long strips of flesh from them, and used them for bayonet practice. At least one hundred men reportedly had their eyes gouged out and their noses and ears hacked off before being set on fire. Another group of two hundred Chinese soldiers and civilians were stripped naked, tied to columns and doors of a school, and then stabbed by "zhuizi"—special needles with handles on them—in hundreds of points along their bodies,*

> *including their mouths, throats, and eyes....The Japanese subjected large crowds of victims to mass incineration. In Hsiakwan [along the Yangtze] a Japanese soldier bound Chinese captives together, ten at a time, and pushed them into a pit, where they were sprayed with gasoline and ignited. The Japanese held grotesque killing contests, including "a competition to determine who could kill the fastest." As one soldier stood sentinel with a machine gun, ready to mow down anyone who tried to bolt, the eight other soldiers split up into pairs to form four separate teams. In each team, one soldier beheaded prisoners with a sword while the other picked up heads and tossed them aside in a pile. The prisoners stood frozen in silence and terror as their countrymen dropped, one by one.*

And, of course, the atrocity is called the Rape of Nanjing because of the widespread sexual assaults that took place in the city. Tens of thousands of women and girls were assaulted, many of them being killed afterward or in the process of being raped. This included girls less than ten and women over seventy.

There is more that could be talked about, but you get the idea. Adding insult to injury is that the vast majority of the perpetrators that survived the war went unpunished. There are a number of reasons for that. First, most Japanese who were left in China when the war ended were transported back to Japan. Second, many of the people who could identify war criminals had either died during the war or could not be found immediately afterward, and if they could be found, most Chinese had more immediate problems to solve, like the Chinese Civil War and the Communist takeover. Third, in the years after the war, the United States and the government of Chiang Kai-shek in Taiwan needed the Japanese as an ally against the People's Republic of China, which was overseen by Mao Zedong, and so, many Japanese war criminals, including those who had committed crimes against Americans, went unpunished. In the 1990s, after Iris Chang's book was published, the Chinese government in Beijing accelerating its move toward free enterprise and needed Japanese expertise and its markets; therefore, it did not want to anger their new business partner since many of the men in charge of Japanese companies in the 1990s were in their seventies, and many had seen action in China. Suffice it to say that the vast majority of Japanese who committed crimes in Nanjing (and China in general) went unpunished, though the commanding Japanese general, Iwane Matsui, survived the war and was put on trial and executed for war crimes in 1948.

However, the massacre in Nanjing had one positive effect: it strengthened Chinese resolve to fight the Japanese. After the initial seizure of much of coastal China and its cities between 1937 and 1938, the fighting between the Chinese and Japanese settled into a costly series of smaller battles, guerrilla war campaigns on the part of the Chinese (especially the Communists), and search and destroy missions on the part of the Japanese. This situation lasted until 1944 when, buoyed by massive amounts of Allied aid coming over the Himalayas and the Burma Road into southern China, both the Communists and Nationalists (sometimes in concert, sometimes separately) began a more aggressive campaign, especially in southern/south-central China.

Until then, however, it began to look as if the Japanese might take over the entire country, but even within Japan, doubts began to creep in about its ability to defeat the enemy. As the war went on, many began to believe that Japan had bitten off far more than it could chew in its attack on China. After all, China was huge. It was also the most populous nation in the world, meaning the Chinese had a virtually inexhaustible supply of men, and they could simply retreat farther into the hinterlands of central and western China where the Japanese could not reach them, at least not with ease and not without stretching their already tenuous supply lines even further.

These doubts on the part of many in Japan (even within parts of the army, which was mostly rabid for Chinese conquest) really began in the spring of 1938 when they engaged the Chinese in the Battle of Tai'erzhuang.

Chapter 8 – They Were Expendable

As some might know, the title of this chapter is the name of a famous book and movie about the experience of American PT boats' commanders and crews during World War II, but the real "expendables" were a group of Chinese soldiers who decided that their own lives were less important than defeating the Japanese.

In late March 1938, the Japanese wished to solidify their hold on northern China, and to do this, they needed to take the city of Xuzhou and the area around it. Xuzhou lay between the Jiangsu province on the coast (which contained Shanghai and Nanjing), the Henan province to the west, where there were sizable Communist forces, and lay astride an important railway and canal system linking the north to the south.

Leading into the populous city of Xuzhou itself was the smaller city of Tai'erzhuang. The city itself lay on the eastern side of the Grand Canal (the ancient and important waterway that transported many of the goods of eastern China), and it was also a key point along an important local railway. The control of Tai'erzhuang was important to both sides. For the Japanese, control of the area would allow them to move in many directions, including in the direction of the city of Wuhan, then a hub of Nationalist activity and troop concentrations.

Strangely enough, however, the battle that was to come came at a time when the Japanese government, including Emperor Hirohito, declared that the offensive operations in China should be halted for at least a year in order to consolidate gains and reinforce troops and their new holdings. But, once again, the Japanese forces in China disregarded orders from above, which is interesting considering the emphasis the Japanese training officers placed on obeying the emperor at all times. However, they were fresh from a major victory in Nanjing and wanted to pursue the fleeing Chinese and engage them in something the Japanese were obsessed with throughout the war, the idea of the "decisive battle," the one battle that would win the war.

The Japanese force moving on the Xuzhou/Tai'erzhuang area came from three directions: north, east, and south. Each prong of the Japanese force was one division in strength but augmented by smaller units. These troops amounted to approximately 40,000 to 75,000 men and around 80 tanks.

The Chinese forces confronting them were a mixed bag of trained and untrained, as well as well-equipped and poorly equipped, soldiers as so many of the Chinese units were at the start of the war, and to make matters worse, they were commanded by rival generals, many of whom had been enemies during the Warlord Era of the 1910s and late 1920s. In addition to the animosity they felt toward each other, which they did try to set aside, many of the generals were filled with disdain for the troops of one another, with regional rivalries and stereotypes playing a role. Opium addiction was also rampant through the ranks. To put it simply, the

Chinese troops were a mess. Yet, in the upcoming Battle of Tai'erzhuang, they were not only victorious, but they also made the name of the town a rallying cry for the Chinese people.

Tai'erzhuang itself was an old city, consisting of a maze of cobblestone streets, stone walls, and cobbled houses linked by a maze of alleyways. Ancient watchtowers and gates were used to observe and resist the Japanese. On one side of the town was the Grand Canal, and on the other sat the railway. Tai'erzhuang was made to be defended, and it needed to be defended to protect Chinese supply lines that moved in all directions.

Most of Tai'erzhuang's residents had fled before the battle started on March 20th, 1938, with a sudden Japanese advance that hoped to stun the defenders and make them retreat, leaving the door to the populous city of Xuzhou open. This failed, and from the 21st to the 24th, the Japanese bombed the city and launched a number of small attacks in conjunction with the bombers.

By March 27th, about half of the Chinese defenders of Tai'erzhuang had been killed or wounded, but under the leadership of Lieutenant General Chi Fengcheng, the Chinese rallied and began to engage the Japanese in close-quarter street fights. This was done to counter the Japanese superiority in artillery and air power. Much of the fighting also took place at night, and the Chinese became adept at infiltration tactics, showing up behind and within Japanese lines to engage them in close combat, much of it hand-to-hand. Today in Tai'erzhuang, a number of memorials exist. In the photo of the one below, you can see Chinese soldiers carrying machete-like knives, which many were equipped with.

Within the city, the battle became a brutal stalemate of street fights. In the West, some of the defenders have become known as "the expendables," but a good translation of the Chinese name is "the dare to die corps," which is a polite way to say "suicide squad." As the fighting became more brutal, and because the Chinese knew that surrendering to the Japanese was likely a fate worse than death, many of them were willing and, in many cases, eager to commit suicide if it meant they could take some Japanese down with them. This was especially true when the Japanese tried to bring in their tanks against the Chinese, who lacked anti-tank weapons of any kind, unless one counts the suicide vests made from grenades, which were detonated by Chinese troops when they managed to get close enough or under Japanese tanks.

Inside the city, a brutal close combat fight was going on. Outside the city, the Chinese, taking advantage of both the terrain and the Japanese men's underestimation of them, brought in additional troops to surround the city and the Japanese troops there. By April 3rd, the Japanese troops in the city had been cornered, and the repeated attempts by Japanese units to break through and relieve the city had failed. By April 6th, 1938, what Japanese forces remained in the city were taken prisoner (nearly 800), and the Chinese got their hands on significant numbers of tanks and artillery, which would aid them in the time to come.

The Battle of Tai'erzhuang, which officially ended on April 7th, was a shock to the Japanese, who had firmly believed they were invincible. In Japan itself, great effort was taken to keep the news of the defeat out of the press, and most Japanese never heard of it—even within parts of the military.

For the Chinese, the victory at Tai'erzhuang was something they could rally around. It showed that their soldiers were capable of beating the Japanese and that their generals, at least some of them, were capable of leading men in battle.

Chapter 9 – The War Drags On

Sadly, most people in the West and many in Japan have forgotten about the Second Sino-Japanese War. If they know anything about it at all, it is likely about the Rape of Nanjing, the Marco Polo Bridge Incident, or the capture of Shanghai (and the latter one probably because of the Steven Spielberg movie *Empire of the Sun* (1987).

One of the most overlooked battles of the Second Sino-Japanese War is the Battle of Wuhan, where an estimated 1.2 million people on both sides lost their lives. That is about the same number as the Battles of Stalingrad and Leningrad and more than the Battle of Berlin in 1945.

Wuhan is located in the Hubei province, and the fighting there in 1938 took place not only in the city but also in the surrounding area. Hubei province is landlocked and links coastal provinces with western provinces. It is also important in any north-south movement. For those of you familiar with the American Civil War, the Hubei province is much like Tennessee was in the 1860s, a hub of traffic, supplies, and men moving in all directions of the compass. After the fall of Nanjing, Wuhan became China's capital in all but name, at least for a short time.

The Japanese wanted to take the area in June 1938, but a variety of problems confronted them. Firstly, it was becoming apparent to the Japanese government that the war in China was going to take far longer than original estimates. Already the Japanese economy was suffering from its wartime exertions, and this was before its declaration of war against the United States.

Manpower that normally would have been in the workforce was being diverted to the military. Spending, which had already gotten almost out of control, continued to increase. This increased the national debt and began to cause inflation. In response, the Japanese government put the entire country on a war footing, including the economy.

In China itself, the Japanese advance toward Wuhan was slowed by a monumental decision on the part of Chiang Kai-shek. Under pressure from his advisors, he ordered the dams on the Yangtze River to be demolished in order to flood the area and slow down the Japanese advance, which it did. It also cost about 800,000 Chinese lives due to drowning, famine from the loss of crops, and disease.

The Japanese were able to bring almost 400,000 men into the battle, along with several hundred aircraft and over 100 naval vessels in the Yangtze River and its tributaries. The naval vessels helped the Japanese prevent reinforcement and resupply of Chinese forces, especially in the city of Wuhan itself.

The Chinese, on the other hand, had an estimated two million men in this key area and approximately one million in Wuhan and its environs. Once again, these units were a mixed bag of quality units and poorly led, motivated, trained, and supplied militia and regular army units, which were slowly improving throughout the many phases of the war.

The battle itself lasted from June to October and encompassed many forms of combat, including the amphibious landings that began the battle, tank battles, and chemical attacks, the latter which were by the Japanese.

The Battle of Wuhan was essentially a series of battles fought over the course of months. Before the battle began, an intense air battle took place, known in Chinese military history as the "2.18 Air Battle" for the date on which it was fought, February 18th. And to the surprise of the Japanese, it ended with a Chinese victory. Another major air battle, involving hundreds of planes over the course of one day, was the "4.29 Air Battle," which was launched by the Japanese to celebrate the emperor's birthday.

The Battle of Wuhan began in earnest on June 15th, 1938, when the Japanese captured the city of Anqing. A few days later, the Japanese made an amphibious landing in two places that forced the Chinese to retreat. Over the course of the next few weeks, the Japanese used their naval forces to navigate the rivers and canals in the Wuhan area to their advantage, and for the first phase of the battle, things went well for the Japanese. In August, however, the Chinese resistance began to stiffen.

As was the story for most of the war, the Japanese found themselves outnumbered, and the Chinese found themselves outgunned. An American military observer with the Chinese estimated the strength of a typical Chinese division at one-third to one-twelfth that of the typical Japanese division. Thinking mathematically, if this was the case, then that means that one hundred Chinese divisions were often equal to only twelve Japanese divisions.

The Japanese knew this, and they also had good intelligence for most of the war. Oftentimes, they would successfully follow the rules of war set down by the, ironically, Chinese warrior Sun Tzu, the main one being strike hard where the enemy is weakest. This meant that oftentimes the Japanese would subject the weakest or most demoralized Chinese units to the heaviest shelling and the heaviest attacks from the air. Besides hopefully defeating their enemy and forcing them to retreat, a bonus would be if these poorer Chinese units panicked, as it would sow fear into the population at large and other Chinese formations in the area.

One of the other issues with the Chinese were the rivalries and suspicions between generals and between Chiang Kai-shek and his subordinates. Chiang had come to power through a series of political maneuvers, and while he was the strongest of the Chinese warlords and was recognized as the man in charge, that didn't mean his generals didn't scheme, and it also didn't mean that he wasn't paranoid when he had no reason to be.

This often led to orders going out to the Chinese units led by Chiang's rivals that were designed to weaken them and/or make them look bad. In contrast, though they played a minor role in the Battle of Wuhan, the Communists, before and during the war, were more democratic in their choice of leadership. Mao Zedong had assumed leadership in the early 1930s, but when things went against the Communists, he was removed from many of his positions. Later, when infighting and indecision filled the Communist ranks, Mao successfully got himself placed back in power.

Though the floods stalled the Japanese advance on the Wuhan area, it also gave them time to consolidate their forces and prepare. After the fall of Anqing, the Chinese set up an elaborate defensive line between the cities of Anqing and Jiujiang at the railroad junction in Madang. Unfortunately, this defensive line was successfully outflanked, and the Japanese captured Jiujiang. Sadly, what the Chinese feared would happen did: the enemy slaughtered many of the remaining thousands of civilians in the city.

The Chinese had strong units under General Bai Chongxi about 100 miles to the north of the Madang position, but through a combination of personal ambitions, jealousies, Japanese movements, and lack of transportation, these troops, which might have changed the face of the battle, remained where they were and were eventually cut off completely. At the end of July, General Bai Chongxi was forced to retreat, and the Kuomintang (the Chinese Nationalist Party) realized the battle was lost, though it carried out an effective fighting retreat that allowed civil servants and industry workers to retreat into the interior of China, where Chiang planned to set up yet another capital, this time at Chongqing. The city of Wuhan itself fell on October 25th, 1938. The Chinese killed and wounded are estimated to be between 600,000 and one million people. The Japanese, who were able to sustain fewer casualties, had an estimated 250,000 killed and wounded.

After the Battle of Wuhan, which officially ended on October 27th with the capture of Hanyang, the lines of the war remained largely the same until late 1944/45, and even at the time of the Japanese surrender, they controlled much of China, as seen below:

Chapter 10 – Horrors Mostly Unknown

In the previous chapter, we mentioned the use of chemical weapons by the Japanese. You also read about the atrocities in Nanjing. These weren't isolated incidents; just look at the institution of the Three Alls Policy—"kill all, burn all, loot all." When a policy such as this is formulated from the top, there are essentially no brakes put on the behavior of subordinates, who now had permission to indulge in their baser instincts against a foe that they had been taught for years was inferior.

At the end of World War II, the Allies (more so the Americans) allowed Emperor Hirohito to retain his throne, albeit with considerably less power than before. The reason for this was to pacify the Japanese population, who the Americans believed would revolt if the emperor was removed since the Japanese believed the emperor was a god on Earth. Aside from the military problems, the Americans needed a cooperative, pacified, and allied Japan in what it knew was the coming struggle against the Soviet Union. Though some of the most egregious war criminals of the Japanese occupation in Asia were caught, tried, and executed, many were not, mainly so that the Americans could keep the Japanese happy.

Twice in the 1970s, Hirohito visited the United States. Both times there were public protests against this, mainly led by veterans of the Pacific War who saw Hirohito not as a dupe of the militarists but as a willing and conscious war criminal. Post-war investigations of Japanese documents proved that Hirohito and another member of the royal family, Prince Naruhiko Higashikuni (who was also the uncle of the emperor), expressly ordered the use of poison gas a stunning 375 times during just the Battle of Wuhan. Just like Emperor Hirohito, though, the prince was never brought to trial.

This investigation and the book that resulted from it, *Dokugasusen Kankei Shiryō* (*Materials on Poison Gas Warfare*), were undertaken after the death of Emperor Hirohito and was written by Japanese historian Yoshiaki Yoshimi. He proved conclusively that not only did the Japanese use chemical warfare in China with regularity, but they also did so with the consent of the highest authorities in the land. Yoshimi also wrote *Sexual Slavery in the Japanese Military during WWII*, which detailed the enslavement of vast numbers of Korean women, as well as the enslavement of tens of thousands of Chinese women and girls.

This leads us to the most brutal and, until recently, the most unknown aspect of Japanese war crimes in China. This is the infamous Unit 731, sometimes known as the Ishii Unit, Ishii Detachment, or Ishii Company), named after its chief, Shirō Ishii, a monster who walked the Earth for far too long. And while what you are about to read is upsetting and graphic in the extreme, perhaps one of the most upsetting things is that Ishii went free because the Americans, who were too ethical to experiment as Ishii had, granted him and his unit immunity at the end of the war. They wanted to learn more about the biological and chemical weapons research he had conducted at his headquarters in Manchukuo in the Pingfang of Harbin, the largest city in Manchukuo. The Soviets, however, did capture a number of Unit 731 members and sentenced them to lengthy terms in the Gulag system of concentration camps. Those that survived were repatriated to Japan in 1956 in a move to improve relations between the two countries.

Shirō Ishii was born in 1892 into a middle-class family and studied medicine at Kyoto Imperial University. In 1921, he joined the army as a surgeon but continued his studies in Tokyo, where he both impressed his superiors and cultivated contacts in high places. Early in his career, Ishii became fascinated by the potential of biological and chemical weapons, and he was granted permission to tour Europe to do research on these subjects in the former combatants of World War I. Over the span of two years, Ishii learned much about chemical warfare and the possibilities of biological weapons and warfare.

Shirō Ishii
https://commons.wikimedia.org/wiki/File:Shiro-ishii.jpg

By 1935, Ishii had established himself in Japan as the leader in chemical weapons research and was made a lieutenant colonel. At the beginning of August 1936, he was given permission to form Unit 731 (a codename with no bearing on the unit's work, as its official name was No. 731 Water Purification Unit) in Manchukuo/Manchuria.

Almost immediately, Ishii and his comrades, notably Dr. Hisato Yoshimura, began to break all the recognized rules and ethics of modern medicine. Like the Nazi doctors did in the 1940s, Ishii, Yoshimura, and others carried out experiments so brutal that they belong in the pages of a horror novel, not in history books.

It is not known for sure how many victims Unit 731 claimed in the Chinese countryside, but by their own words and in documents found at the end of the war, Unit 731's men distributed fleas carrying bubonic plague in various places in the Chinese countryside near the city of Changde. It is estimated that, as a result, some 250,000 people died miserably from the same Black Death that had ravaged Europe in the 14th century. They also spread cholera, botulism, and smallpox in civilian areas, as well as deliberately infected prisoners. These prisoners were mostly Chinese who were picked at random from prisons or simply off the streets, but there was also a lesser percentage of Russians, Mongols, and Koreans. There was a small number of Allied prisoners, mostly Americans whose bombers had crashed in China after raiding Japan.

Just as the Germans did in the Holocaust, the Japanese of Unit 731 used euphemisms to both hide their crimes and to inure their men to the torturing of their victims. In the death camps of Poland, the Jewish and other Nazi victims were "cargo," which received "special treatment" (meaning gassing). At Unit 731's compound in Manchukuo, the victims were known and referred to as "logs"—pieces of wood to be experimented upon, cut up, and burned.

In addition to infecting more than 3,000 people with diseases, Ishii and the men of Unit 731 often killed them before the disease could, but it was not out of mercy. In order to study the progress of the disease, the Japanese often performed autopsies on their "logs," even before they were dead. What's more, they did this without anesthesia.

Whether or not the grim nature of their work inured them to the suffering cries of their victims is sort of a moot point (unless you're a criminologist or psychologist), but as time went on, the men of Unit 731 decided they would carry out experiments far exceeding what most people can imagine. In at least one case, one prisoner was given a transfusion; as his own blood was drained out of him, he was given horse blood. He died in agony.

Other experiments included exposing men to chemical and fire burns to test the limits of human endurance and survivability, as well as the same type of air-pressure experiments conducted by Nazi doctors, in which prisoners were put into pressure chambers and exposed to low pressure until they literally exploded. They were also injected with seawater, placed in centrifuges and spun until they died, and exposed to lethal amounts of X-rays (sometimes all at one time). One team at Unit 731 seemed to enjoy performing operations that had no medical or research purposes at all, even given the extreme tenuousness of that which already went on at the camp—they sometimes even amputated limbs and attached them to other areas of the body. Other horrors included electrocution, drowning, and weapons testing on human bodies.

Women prisoners were repeatedly raped, sometimes by other prisoners known to be carrying STDs or having been deliberately infected with them. Other women were deliberately impregnated and then tortured to see if the fetus would live. Those babies that were not killed in this manner were aborted or killed shortly after birth.

Hisato Yoshimura was responsible for testing human reaction and endurance to extreme cold. Men, women, and children were frozen and intentionally allowed to develop gangrene through frostbite. One of the experiments these poor people endured (aside from the extreme pain of frostbite and gangrene) was to be prodded and cut by surgical instruments to test their pain level while frozen or "thawed." Limbs were doused in freezing water and exposed to the freezing air of Manchukuo in winter. The Japanese would then attempt to "thaw" them with fire. The list of the atrocities committed at this unit is too long to continue.

Those at the top knew about Unit 731. The unit could not have operated in areas under Japanese control without that kind of knowledge since Japanese troops needed to avoid infected areas, and the prisoners were brought in from other areas under Japanese control.

At the end of the war, Ishii came up with a plan that he and others thought might turn the tide of war: infecting the United States' West Coast with the same type of plague-infected fleas that they had dropped in China. Operation Cherry Blossoms at Night luckily never came to fruition, as the war was nearing its end by the time they thought about putting it into action.

Ishii and most members of Unit 731 were granted immunity. The Japanese press and government never spoke of it, and it had not been until the last thirty years that it has been discussed with any great publicity in China. Today, visitors can visit the Unit 731 compound, which is now a memorial.

Unit 731 Camp
https://commons.wikimedia.org/wiki/File:Unit_731_-_Complex.jpg

It should not be thought that the atrocities during this conflict went only one way. There were many instances of Japanese troops being massacred and tortured after they were captured and after the war ended. While this doesn't excuse this type of behavior in any way whatsoever, it should be noted that any Chinese war crimes came as random actions and not as part of any government policy, such as the "Three Alls."

Chapter 11 – Friends

In 1940, the Japanese invaded French Indochina (today's Vietnam), taking advantage of the weakness of the French in the area after the Nazi occupation of their home country. This was done in conjunction with a Japanese offensive in southern China and a major engagement with the Chinese in the Guangxi province, which borders northernmost Vietnam and the South China Sea. While the battle against the Chinese was actually a defeat for the Japanese, they managed to move into Vietnam and add that territory to their empire.

The Battle of South Guangxi and the invasion of Vietnam had a number of consequences. From a global perspective, it put Japan on a direct path to war with the United States. From a localized perspective (albeit a large one), the Chinese, though they won the Battle of South Guangxi militarily and forced the Japanese to retreat into fortified coastal areas there, the concurrent Japanese invasion of Vietnam cut off an important supply route into the territories under their control. Any supplies that came into China would have to come from either the Soviet

Union (which did send limited amounts) or from the area of British India or Burma. Either route was exceedingly difficult.

The Chinese, not being able to drive the Japanese from their own country, were not able to do anything to aid the French (or later the Vietnamese) in their struggle against the Japanese. The Japanese were too strong at sea and able to resupply their forces in Vietnam at will.

The other consequence of the Japanese invasion of Indochina was to bring the United States into political, economic, and, eventually, military conflicts with Japan, and it also caused an increasing number of isolationists in the United States to begin to side against Japan (and slowly, its ally, Germany).

The Japanese takeover of Vietnam was relatively bloodless. Though there were occasional small battles between French troops who defied orders coming from the new collaborationist government in France, most of the troops there moved aside when the Japanese moved in. In the beginning, many Vietnamese were duped (as others were as the war spread) by Japanese propaganda, which put forward the idea that they were fighting the Europeans for their Asian brothers "Asia for Asiatics" was their slogan. All the people had to do was see how the Japanese treated the Koreans and Chinese for them to know that the "Asiatics" in the slogan meant only the Japanese. As brutal Japanese rule fell on Vietnam, the Vietnamese began a guerrilla war against them.

The United States, already angered by Japanese actions in China (which had included some "accidental" attacks on American gunboats in Chinese rivers, which were there to protect their concessions and interests and that were sometimes there at the request of Chiang Kai-shek's government), had threatened the Japanese with economic sanctions if they were to take any aggressive action in Indochina. When they did, the Americans virtually stopped all trade with Japan, especially that involving steel, coal, and oil.

As was mentioned earlier in this book, the Japanese military machine was dependent on all three of these resources coming from the United States. Without them, virtually all Japanese military activity would cease.

Pushed into a corner of their own making, the Japanese made plans not only to attack the US fleet at Pearl Harbor but also to drive the Americans from the eastern Pacific completely. They would attack the US territories of the Philippines, Guam, and Wake Island, among others. While they were at it, the Japanese would attempt to defeat another threat, Great Britain, an ally of the United States that kept a sizable fleet in the Pacific to protect their territories in Hong Kong, Singapore, and Malaysia.

As we all know, in the short term, the Japanese were successful. The US was driven out of the eastern Pacific, the British were defeated, and the US fleet took incredible damage at Pearl Harbor.

Another byproduct of the Japanese attack was to allow US President Franklin Delano Roosevelt to send much more aid to China. While many in the United States and US Congress were friends of the Chinese and sympathized with them, many in the country were wary of getting involved in a war so far away. When the Japanese attacked the US directly, though, the gloves came off.

Before Pearl Harbor, President Franklin Roosevelt secretly authorized a group of fighter pilots and crewmen to fight the Japanese in China, either secretly or at least under ostensible Chinese command. This was the American Volunteer Group (the AVG), or more famously known as the Flying Tigers.

The AVG was under the direct command of retired American army officer Claire Chennault, who had essentially been forced out of the Army Air Corps because of his difficult nature and his bad hearing. Chennault was an accomplished pilot and had studied fighter tactics for some time, including being the head of an aerobatic team designed to perfect and display pursuit tactics and maneuvers. When he retired, he sought greener pastures in China, where, in the 1930s, the Chinese were hiring as many foreign military experts as it could to help in its fight against the Japanese. Chennault became one of a handful of American pilots, both civilian and ex-military, who helped the Chinese air force beginning in 1937. By 1938, Chennault was in charge of training all the foreign pilots helping the Chinese (with the exception of a number of Soviets, who operated secretly against the Japanese until they were recalled for the coming fight against Finland in 1939 and what was expected to be a coming war with Hitler).

Chennault's immediate superior was none other than the wife of the Generalissimo, Soong Mei-ling, also known as Madame Chiang. Though she rubbed many people the wrong way, Madame Chiang, with the contacts of her wealthy family and Chiang behind her, could also be charming when she wished to be, and when the time came, her influence in Washington would become very useful.

In the fall of 1939, Chennault and four high-ranking Chinese officers went on a mission for Chiang Kai-shek to the United States. By this time, the Chinese air force, which had previously fought well on occasion, although it was both outgunned and lacked the skill of the Japanese, was in disarray, a polite way of saying "almost gone." Chiang sent Chennault to the US in late 1940 to see if he could secure both funding, planes, and pilots for a large formation of American squadrons to take on the enemy.

Madame Chiang's brother, an influential banker that went by the name T.V. Soong, was already in Washington lobbying Roosevelt to support a plan that saw American pilots manning Boeing B-17 bombers with Chinese air force markings while bombing Tokyo. Coincidentally, Soong's campaign reached its peak in the fall/winter of 1940, just before the

Japanese attack on Pearl Harbor. This was when Chennault and his party arrived.

Out of the meetings they had with American officials, the AVG was born. There would be no bombing of Tokyo, but Chennault was given the green light to recruit American pilots to go to China to fight the Japanese. Almost everyone involved believed that it was just a matter of time before the Americans were at war with Japan, and fighting the Japanese in China would give the American pilots experience that they could then convey to the US Air Force when war did break out. It happened exactly that way, too. Among the pilots of the AVG who later returned to teach and fly for their home country was Gregory "Pappy" Boyington, the founder of the famous "Black Sheep" Marine squadron and one of the leading aces of the Pacific War.

By the time the AVG became active in China, the war had broken out between the US and Japan, but most of the pilots and crew that signed on remained in China. They had not only signed contracts, but they also knew it was likely going to be a long time before they had an opportunity to fly in combat if they went back home.

Of course, the Flying Tigers are known for their famous Curtiss P-40 Warhawks with a shark's mouth painted on the front. Though the Tigers are the best-known group that flew planes painted with a shark's mouth, it was originally a German idea, which was adopted by the British and then by the AVG, who liked the distinctive look. The mouth also singled out the group, who, while supposedly flying in the guise of Chinese pilots, knew the Japanese would soon recognize them for what they were—Americans in Chinese-marked planes.

The AVG produced nineteen aces (men with five or more enemy planes shot down). While the number of Americans flying at any one time was about sixty, they seemed to number far more, as their planes, their panache, their skill, and the distinctive flying jackets with the "flying tiger" on the back all made them seem larger than life.

Another thing that made them larger than life was their record. While there are a variety of numbers floating about concerning the kills of the Flying Tigers (most of the confusion stems from figures in aerial combat versus planes destroyed on the ground), for our purposes, we are going to follow aviation expert and Flying Tiger member Erik Shilling's numbers: 297 aircraft destroyed (160 in combat, 137 on the ground) with a loss of 19 men. Yes, nineteen. And of those nineteen, only four were shot down. The rest were killed in crashes or were crewmen or pilots caught in Japanese attacks on airbases. The Japanese reported over 500 Flying Tigers being shot down; however, there were never that many men in the AVG for all the years they fought.

Of course, the Flying Tigers were only the most famous of a massive effort on the part of the United States and the United Kingdom to supply the Chinese in their fight against the Japanese. The two most famous routes into the country were called the Hump and the Burma Road.

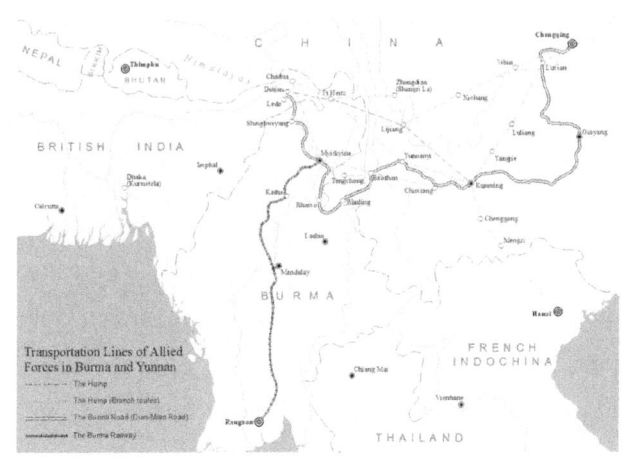

Map showing the Hump route and the Burma Road(s).
SY, CC BY-SA 4.0 <https://creativecommons.org/licenses/by-sa/4.0>, via Wikimedia Commons https://commons.wikimedia.org/wiki/File:The_Hump_and_Burma_Road.png

The Hump was the nickname for something a little bigger: the highest mountain range in the world, the Himalayas. The Burma Road is also a slight misnomer, for the "road" that was used to bring supplies from British India into Burma and then into China was actually a number of routes and was more savage jungle path than road. Each of these routes was fraught with danger, and many men lost their lives trying to help the Chinese.

Flying out of India, American and British pilots, mostly piloting American Douglas DC-3s (known in the military as C-47s), had to strain their aircraft and themselves to the utmost to fly over the peaks of the Himalayas. Actually, when fully loaded, the C-47s could not fly over the mountains but had to find a way *through* them, perhaps an even more daunting proposition. Freezing temperatures and high winds took a high toll, as can be expected. Sometimes the losses were so high and/or the weather so bad that supplies had to be halted for some time. Over the course of the war, some 1,200 Allied airmen perished flying over the Hump, with a loss of 700 planes. Of those 1,200 men, 500 were never accounted for. Many men, knowing that if they survived a crash they would likely perish due to the elements or be captured by the Japanese (who would torture them first), kept one bullet ready for themselves.

At its peak, there were planes flying over the Hump every two minutes, so vital was their mission. Some 84,000 men and women (the latter mostly nurses and clerical staff) worked to deliver over 10,000 tons of supplies a month. It should not be forgotten that more than two million Indian and Chinese laborers cut out the amazing number of airfields needed, mostly by hand. Obviously, the type of supplies coming this way was limited—no tanks or heavy guns were being flown over the Hump. That was one of the reasons for the Burma Road.

As mentioned above, the Burma Road was not a single road but a series of them linking British-controlled ports in southern Burma with southern China. The road was actually in use before the British or the US was at war with Japan. It operated from 1937/1938 to 1942. For a period of time in 1940, Japanese threats and diplomatic pressure caused the British to close the road for a period of three months, but they reopened it after pleas from China.

This picture is often mistaken for part of the Burma Road, but it lies in China. However, this is how much of the route looked.
https://commons.wikimedia.org/wiki/File:Ledo_%26_Burma_Roads,_Assam,_Burma,_China._1944-45_-_NARA_-_292561.jpg

The 717 miles of the Burma Road allowed the British to bring in hundreds of thousands of tons of supplies until 1942, when the Japanese invaded Burma itself, mostly to shut down the Burma Road supply route. In early 1945, after the Japanese had been pushed out of Burma, the road was reopened until the war officially ended.

By the end of the war, the United States alone had sent more than 1.6 billion dollars in aid to China. In 2019, that would be the equivalent of nearly 30 billion dollars.

Conclusion – The End of the War

After the Battle of Wuhan in 1938, the Chinese Nationalists moved their capital to the inland city of Chongqing (then known in the West as Chunking). By that time, their forces were depleted and badly in need of the supplies mentioned in the prior chapter. Still, with some exceptions, morale was relatively high. Despite losing a sizable portion of the eastern part of their country, especially the coastal regions, the Chinese had evidence that they could defeat the Japanese in battle. Given the opportunity to regroup and be better trained and supplied on a regular basis (China lacked the industrial base and resources to resupply themselves on anything but a small scale), the Chinese were confident that they could defeat the Japanese.

There was ample reason to believe this, as well as ample reason to doubt it.

On the positive side, the Chinese had shown that when well-armed and well-led, they could defeat the Japanese. The Chinese and Allied leadership also knew, as the Japanese were learning, that it would be almost impossible for the Japanese to conquer the entire country, and if they did not conquer the entire country, then they were likely to lose the war. The Chinese population was too great, their possible supply routes too many, and the Chinese allies too rich (and growing more powerful every day). The longer the war went on, the higher the likelihood of a Japanese defeat grew.

In the late 1960s, the Soviet Union and China fought a brief border war against each other. The reasons for this conflict are immaterial here, but at the time, there was a joke that went around the leadership of the US Armed Forces: "On the first day, the Soviets killed a million Chinese. On the second, two million. On the third, three million. On the fourth day, the Soviets surrendered." The Chinese population and its military potential were just too great for the Japanese to win.

Historians suggest that there were 22 major battles of the Second Sino-Japanese War. Most of the important ones have been cited in this book already. After 1938, the battles that took place did not materially change the situation on the ground, despite some of them being Chinese victories. The Japanese, because of their advantages in air and naval power, still controlled vast swathes of the most populous parts of China, mainly its coastline, and it remained in control of them until the war ended.

However, over the course of the rest of the war, not only were large and costly battles fought (both in terms of manpower and civilian casualties), but an endless series of smaller battles took place, as well as countless guerrilla raids and campaigns, mostly undertaken by the Communists, who gained popularity throughout the war. Just as the Americans were to experience in Vietnam some 25 years later, the Japanese were the victims of a constant, grinding guerrilla campaign that took place not only in the border areas between the two forces but also within the Chinese cities, towns, and countryside under Japanese control. Many of the civilian casualties of the war did not come as a result of combat but in retribution for the myriad number of attacks on Japanese troops and installations. To be fair, many of the Japanese captured in these small battles and in the larger ones as well found that it was likely better that they had died in battle. Yes, for those of you who believe the Japanese killed themselves rather than surrender, many, especially toward the end of the war, were captured.

In the summer and fall of 1944, there was one "last hurrah" for the Japanese in China. The Battle of Changsha was undertaken to connect the Japanese controlled territories from Korea through Manchuria/Manchukuo and uniting the many Japanese enclaves in southern coastal China. This battle ended in a Japanese victory, through the three-month-long battle claimed tens of thousands of Japanese lives.

The battle was fought around the provincial capital of Hunan, Changsha, but it was, in reality, a series of battles fought over a wide area, much like the Battle of Wuhan. Chinese casualties were about 100,000 compared to Japanese losses of about 70,000; however, the Chinese could more easily "afford" them. The Japanese could not. Many of the Japanese troops fighting in this battle had come at a time when Japanese naval and transport strength were needed in the Pacific to fight the Americans, a number that was already dwindling rapidly because Japan was losing that fight. As a result, many of the almost half million men sent to fight in the Battle of Changsha were stranded in China when they were needed desperately elsewhere.

When the Americans dropped the two atomic bombs on Japan in August 1945, their ally, the Soviet Union, fulfilled an agreement they had made earlier in the war and declared war on Japan. Within a very short time, the Japanese armies in northern China and Manchuria were defeated by a combination of Soviet and Chinese Communist troops.

For its part, the US and its Nationalist Chinese armies moved as quickly as they could into the areas of coastal China that were previously occupied by the Japanese. They also moved into southern Korea as the Soviets moved into the north.

All of this helped to set the stage for a resumption of the war between the Communists and Nationalists of China that had taken place in the time between the Japanese invasion of Manchuria and its attack at the Marco Polo Bridge. The conflict between the motivated Communists and the increasingly demoralized, corrupt, and divided Nationalists began almost right away, and it only increased in intensity until the final defeat of Chiang Kai-shek's government and its escape to Taiwan.

Part 2: The Rape of Nanking

The Nanjing Massacre That Occurred during the Second Sino-Japanese War

Introduction

The Rape of Nanjing, also known as the Nanjing Massacre or the Nanking Massacre, was one of the most horrific atrocities of World War II, and it was perpetrated by the Japanese against the people of China who lived in the capital Nanjing. While most people have heard of the Holocaust, the history of the atrocities perpetrated in the East is far less known and is not often covered in schools. Similar to the Holocaust, the lives of citizens were completely disregarded as the invading Japanese military used them for a wide range of unethical actions. Reported activity includes experiments and competitions, with the competitions including members of the Japanese seeing who could kill the most people the fastest.

Unlike the Holocaust, the Nanjing Massacre only lasted six weeks, starting from the day the Japanese invaded the capital on December 13th, 1937. It is unknown exactly how many people were murdered during this time, but the estimates range from 40,000 unarmed combatants and civilians to more than 300,000. The invaders also sexually assaulted their victims. Like the Nazis, the Japanese stole from their victims as well, leaving the capital with valuables and priceless works of art.

It is difficult to know exactly what happened. Over the roughly six-week period, documents were kept by people who were in the city at the time, as well as by Japanese journalists. However, many of the documents were classified as secret by the Japanese government and stored so that the atrocities were not well known among the Japanese people. They were unable to keep other documents written by the Chinese and Westerners, though, so word spread throughout the rest of the world about what had happened. Before their final surrender, the Japanese military destroyed most of the documentation that they had kept on what happened, making it impossible to know exactly how many people were killed.

While it is easy to compare the Rape of Nanjing to the Holocaust, there are many notable differences as well, particularly in terms of how much is known. One of the reasons so much is known about the Holocaust is that the Allies actually walked into the concentration camps and saw the horrors that had been perpetrated against the people who were imprisoned within them. There were survivors who were able to tell the Allied liberators how they had been treated beyond the obvious starvation. People did survive the horrors of the Rape of Nanjing, but it had been more than seven years since the events of the atrocity, so most of the evidence of the horrors had already been destroyed. Many survivors were also not willing to relive the experience. In addition, those who were willing to talk about it did not have the kinds of details that people wanted to know, such as how many people were massacred.

Another reason why there isn't as much known about the six weeks of horror is due to the Cold War starting almost as soon as World War II ended. The US had largely been given control of helping to rebuild Japan, and they learned about some of the atrocities. However, they were more concerned with the potential threats posed by communist nations than in looking too far into the atrocity. The Chinese Civil War resumed once World War II ended, but regardless of which side won, the nation was going to be a communist one. Instead of seeking justice for the atrocities committed nearly a decade earlier, the US focused on building up Japan so that it would not fall to the potential threat of communism. That doesn't mean people were not held accountable, but justice was not sought on the same level against Japan as it was against Germany.

With so little attention being given to the Rape of Nanjing in the years following it, the horrors could have been completely forgotten. However, not everything was lost when the Japanese military destroyed much of their documentation. Many images of the military performing horrific acts and the carnage that they left on the beaches and in the city still remain.

War has always resulted in atrocities, but over the last one hundred years, record keeping and technology have made it easier to understand the extent of the horrors war can cause. The events of the Rape of Nanjing still remain a point of contention between Japan and China. The apologies issued by Japan are often seen by the Chinese as being either inadequate or insincere. The fact that some even dispute that it happened, despite the admission by some of the Japanese who were there and the images showing what happened, has further kept the nations from healing or establishing better relationships.

Chapter 1 – A Quick History of Sino-Japanese Relations

The relationship between China and Japan is called Sino-Japanese relations in English-speaking nations. Japan is an island nation located to the east of the main Asian continent, and it has had a unique relationship with the other continental nations. China is a large nation that makes up the majority of the eastern part of the continent. There are several small nations along the eastern border of the continent, including North Korea, South Korea, and Vietnam. Russia also touches the Pacific Ocean, taking up the majority of the northern part of Asia. All of these nations have maintained changing relationships over the centuries, making for a rich and complex history.

The relationship between Japan and China has always been unique. While China has broken apart and merged together over the centuries, Japan is one of the nations that China has never conquered. The conflicts between the two nations have long been a factor in their relationships with other empires and states in the region. However, the First Sino-Japanese War (1894-1895) significantly changed the dynamic between the two nations. Because of the Silk Road, China had strong ties to Europe, including familiarity with their weaponry. Japan had gone through a long period of isolationism, so they were learning about totally new technology. The Japanese quickly adapted, though, and during the short First Sino-Japanese War, Japan established itself as being far more dominant compared to its much larger neighbor.

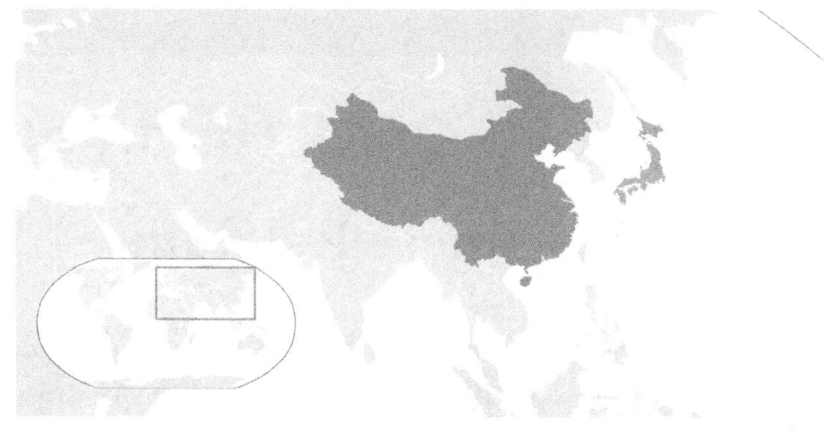

Map of China and Japan
https://commons.wikimedia.org/wiki/File:China_Japan_Locator.png

The First Sino-Japanese War

Both nations had placed claims on parts of what is now modern-day Korea. China had long controlled large portions of the area and relied on it as a client state, particularly because of all of its natural resources, like iron and coal. The land's natural resources were abundant enough to also attract Japan's attention. Japan, an island nation growing into the technology of the time, was seeking to trade with regions that could supply the resources it needed to modernize the country. With Korea being so close and rich in resources, the island nation began to consider ways that would allow it to make use of those resources. However, the territory was under China's control, making trade very limited. In an effort to improve trade, Japan started to encourage Korea to declare itself an independent nation, starting in 1875. The primary objective was to improve its own trade; Japan did not have any humanitarian interests when it helped to push the region to become self-sufficient and independent from Chinese rule. By working directly with a new nation instead of having to work with China, Japan would have been able to establish agreements that were more beneficial to their own self-interests.

Both nations favored different portions of the Korean government, with Japan backing the more radical and forward-looking officials who wanted to make the region more modern. China supported the more traditional officials who wanted to keep things largely the way they had always been. The tension these two nations created within the Korean government began to adversely affect it, and in 1884, the group that wanted to reform the region, the side aligned with the Japanese, made its move to overthrow the Korean government. China had military officials in the region, and they swiftly sent their military in to save the king and support the administration. During the ensuing battle, some Japanese legation members were killed. The only reason that war did not begin between China and Japan at this point was due to a mutual agreement to remove all of their troops, an agreement they reached and signed at the Li-Ito Convention.

Over the next five years, Japan was able to make significant strides in its efforts to modernize the nation. In 1894, the Japanese were feeling considerable national pride at how rapidly they had managed to achieve their goals. This pride seemed to have spread to the younger Korean people, who saw the changes and were inspired. China reacted with apparent apprehension, and they invited the Korean leader of the coup of

1884, Kim Ok-gyun, to Shanghai. Once there, Kim Ok-gyun was assassinated. His body was returned and displayed, likely as a reminder to the Koreans that they were still a part of China.

Japan did not take this obvious affront well, and even its citizens were angered at how China had found a way to go back on the agreement. China had not sent its military into Korea, opting instead to lure a high-profile pro-Japanese figure and assassinate him. That same year, the Tonghak rebellion began, resulting in the Korean king requesting assistance from China to put it down. When China complied, Japan saw this as a violation of the Li-Ito Convention. They sent eight thousand of their own troops. China then responded by sending more troops on the British steamer *Kowshing*, which the Japanese sank. War was inevitable, and it was officially declared on August 1st, 1894. Most of the world expected China to easily defeat Japan. They had been modernizing their nation for much longer, and they were a much larger nation. However, everyone underestimated just how much work Japan had done. Though it was a much smaller and less populous country, it was better prepared for the war. Japan had largely won the war by the beginning of March 1895, as the Japanese quickly executed several overwhelming victories against China, both in the water and on land. They had invaded both Manchuria and the Shandong province, giving them posts that helped them to control the waters. This meant that, for the Chinese, reaching Beijing by sea was much harder, and it was a blow that China could not accept. China sought peace soon after, and the Treaty of Shimonoseki was soon initiated. As a result, Korea was given its independence, although it had to cede the Liaodong Peninsula, the Pescadores, and Taiwan. Japan established itself as a much larger player on the world's stage, having accomplished what most considered to be impossible—easily executing a decisive defeat against the much larger, more historically open China.

Relations Following the War

Having seen that China could be defeated, and by a small nation at that, European nations were inspired to push China for more change. Internally, China began to look to do more to become more modern. Changes were made to the Treaty of Shimonoseki when European nations began to worry about Japan expanding, with Russia (a nation that was just across a small body of water from Japan) playing a large role in pressing for these changes. Russia had long wanted the peninsula that China had been required to give to Japan, and both France and Germany felt that Japan was enough of a threat to warrant relinquishing the lands. Japan ended up selling the region to Russia, but this intervention by the European powers caused some resentment in Japan, especially among the people in the military. Eventually, that resentment caused the Russo-Japanese War (1904-1905) to break out, which ended with another Japanese victory.

By the early part of the 20th century, Japan had established itself as a much more important nation on the global stage. The First Sino-Japanese War resulted in the island nation starting to form its own empire, and the Russo-Japanese War helped to further expand that empire. This inspired the Japanese to attempt to take more lands and take a much more aggressive approach in increasing its influence.

With these two major successes within a decade, a sense of nationalism and superiority began to grow in Japan, particularly within the military. Intellectuals and members of the military began to believe that such quick, decisive victories against two much larger, more powerful nations were a sign that they were destined to control a much larger chunk of the world. The historian Kurakichi Shiratori best explained this sentiment as "Nothing in the world compares to the divine nature of the imperial house and likewise the majesty of our national polity. Here is one great reason for Japan's superiority."

This sentiment is incredibly familiar to anyone who has studied the first half of the 20th century (or any other period in history that deals with empires). Nationalism was spreading across Europe as well, in an equally detrimental way, resulting in the start of World War I. A series of tragedies resulted in nations being dragged one by one into the war until it engulfed all of the European continent. However, because of the empire-building that the European nations had been enacting over the years, nations from around the world were pulled into the fight. France and Great Britain were the primary nations on the one side, while Germany was the primary nation on the opposite side. Russia was not a part of the war for long because the nation fell into a civil war, called the Bolshevik Revolution, which resulted in the assassination of the entire Russian royal family.

When the war first erupted in Europe, both China and Japan saw it as an opportunity to remove European influence from Asia. As a result, both nations declared war on Germany. China had continued to lose lands after the First Sino-Japanese War, but the losses were to European nations (France had a settlement in Shanghai, and England took over Hong Kong). It is likely that they hoped to negotiate with these nations after helping them to beat Germany. However, China had other reasons to declare war on Germany, for the nation had attacked the city of Qingdao in 1897 under the guise of seeking justice for two German missionaries killed in the city.

China offered to help Great Britain, but the offer was declined. It wouldn't be accepted until 1916 that the British prime minister tried to persuade the nation that they needed the help. Japan quickly spoke up, saying that it did not agree with China being so actively involved in the war.

If China was to participate successfully, it would threaten Japan's status in Asia. In an effort to avoid an all-out war with Japan, China decided to send non-military personnel to help with the fight in Britain, France, and Russia (they remained a part of the war in a minor capacity after the Bolsheviks took over the nation). The support staff helped in manufacturing, repairs, and transport.

Japan ended up successfully taking Qingdao in 1915, then issued the Twenty-One Demands to China. This set of demands required that China give up even more land. It is likely that China hoped that its efforts to help Europe would result in reclaiming some of the lost lands.

Toward the end of World War I, the United States finally joined the conflict, and it had a goal of finally resolving the question of which nation would control the disputed areas. China finally made its declaration of war against Germany in 1917 in the hopes of garnering more support from the US once the war ended. By the war's end, China had both the longest-serving and largest contingent of non-European workers in Europe. The Chinese had been planning for the end of the war since 1915, so they were eager to have their representatives push for the restoration of the mainland under their control. Those hopes were quickly dashed, though, as the Paris Peace Conference saw only two seats at the conference given to China, while five were given to Japan. The justification for this was that Japan had actually supplied troops. European nations considered the Twenty-One Demands as something that should be honored in order to resolve the claim to the lands. Of all the nations to attend the Paris Peace Conference, China was the only one that refused to sign the Treaty of Versailles.

As a result of the slight and the perceived rejection of their sovereignty by the most powerful European and North American nations, China began to reevaluate its position. In 1921, this led to the formation of the

Chinese Communist Party and a long civil war. While China entered a long period of turmoil as it tried to find its place in the world, Japan continued to look for ways to take over larger portions of continental Asia.

Chapter 2 – A Brief History of Nanjing

Nanjing (once better known as Nanking) has an extensive history, making it difficult to know how many of the stories that have survived are true and how many are myths. There are two primary stories told about the city. The first indicates that Nanjing is over 2,600 years. The small settlement, which was founded around 571 BCE, developed into a much larger city over the millennia. When people first began settling in the area, they coalesced around Tangyi, a tiny village. Today, this is located on the western side of the city.

The second story of the city's founding places the date around 472 BCE. According to this version, the head of state, Goujian, had the city built near the southwestern area of the modern-day Zhonghua Gate. At that time, the city was known as Yue City. The construction of the city included walls to protect the residents, making it one of the oldest fortified locations in China. It is also the oldest place in modern-day Nanjing (though it took up a much smaller part of the city since it was considerably smaller over two thousand years ago).

It is possible that both of these stories are true, with the main distinction being that it was only a village and that it didn't officially become a city until 472 BCE when the walls were constructed around it.

In 229 CE, King Sun Quan made it the capital of the Kingdom of Wu, though, at the time, the city was named Jianye. Before this time, the capital of the kingdom had been in the Yellow River region. As a result of the shift, the southern part of the kingdom began to thrive and change, attracting a lot more people. It remained the capital of the Kingdom of Wu through five Chinese dynasties. Between 229 and 589 CE, the name was changed from Jianye to Jiankang, though it is unknown when the change became official. During the time when it was called Jiankang, it became the world's largest city, and it was likely the first city to have over one million people. During this time, it would have been comparable to Rome at its height, and it was considered by many to be the cultural center of the world. It was a hub for many industries and trade, including architecture and marine trade. It also saw the development and growth of a number of Asian religions, including Buddhism, Confucianism, and Taoism.

After having prospered over three hundred years, the capital began an inevitable decline; all cities go through decline, but it was rebuilt again later. The primary reason for the city's descent was the presence of separatists, particularly the ones near the capital. The capital was moved, and Jinling (yet another name given to the city) was converted to a prefecture (equivalent to a county). While the city was no longer as prominent, it remained a hub for culture and scholars who wanted to study the empire's history.

After China divided under the period called the Five Dynasties and Ten Kingdoms, Jinling once again became the capital, though only of the region. This time, the focus was on building the three primary pillars of culture: agriculture, art, and commerce.

By the time the Ming dynasty was established in 1368 CE, the city had been renamed Nanjing. Under the first member of the Ming dynasty, Zhu Yuanzhang, the city was made the capital of the dynasty. Though Nanjing was not as populous as it had been a few hundred years earlier, it did become the largest city in the country, with an estimated 700,000 people residing in and around it. This time, though, the city began attracting attention from outside of the country. Students came to Nanjing to study, particularly from Korea, Japan, and Vietnam. Even after the capital was shifted to the port city of Beijing in 1421, Nanjing continued to function as the auxiliary capital. The population once again boomed, and as a result, Nanjing became the world's most populous capital city. It was even compared to the most extravagant European nations by those who traveled between the two continents.

The city continued to experience a boom for several hundred years, becoming a culturally significant place for art and commerce. It became an important part of the silk trade, and it was also the setting for one of the most popular classic Chinese novels, *Hong Lou Meng* (*Dream of the Red Mansions*).

One of the most disgraceful periods for the city occurred as a result of the Opium Wars during the Qing dynasty. The dynasty reached an agreement with Great Britain called the Treaty of Nanjing. This appeared to be a significant loss for the city and China, as the terms set forth in the treaty made China more like a semi-colony of the European nation. It gave Great Britain a much greater say in tariffs, commercial preference, and consular jurisdiction. This is considered to be the beginning of modern China, for it was around this time that the nation began to modernize.

In an effort to make up for the large sums of money that the nation had spent during the Opium Wars, the Chinese government heavily taxed the citizens (or perhaps more accurately to erase the savings, as the nation became more feudalistic following the signing of the treaty). This resulted in peasant wars, as the people felt wronged by the government. During this unrest, the Taiping army saw an opportunity to take control of Nanjing. The army was created by Hong Xiuquan in 1837. He was the son of a peasant family but had received a classical education that taught him about beliefs from around the world. After failing to gain work in the imperial court, Hong became ill, then fell into a coma. Upon waking, he claimed to have had a vision that he was Jesus's younger brother and that he needed to lead people to establish a "Heavenly Kingdom of Great Peace." This was to be done through war with the emperor and those who supported the emperor, especially the military. By 1853, his army was much larger than the emperor's. Hong Xiuquan's men took control of Nanjing, but they were not able to control it for long. The Taiping Rebellion lasted for thirteen years, and when it ended, the Taiping army was finally put down. However, it also proved to be the end of the Qing dynasty.

By 1912, China was reasserting itself on the world stage, having modernized more than most of the other Eastern nations (except for Japan). On the first day of 1912, the Provisional Government of the Republic of China was formed in Nanjing.

The years between 1927 and 1937 are considered to be a golden period for the city because it was when the nation established its major infrastructure, on which most of the city still currently runs. However, it was this prominence, wealth of resources, and cultural importance that made the city a desirable target to the Japanese. With Europe already embroiled in war and Japan having made advances in continental Asia, the Japanese were looking for a place that would give them greater dominance farther inland while also helping to increase their resources. The Japanese thought that if they were able to successfully take Nanjing with its impressive municipal infrastructure, they would establish better footing within China. It would also be a significant blow to the divided Chinese government, as the civil war would have made the large nation too weak to face invasions. The loss of Nanjing would significantly reduce Chinese morale.

Even today, the city plays an important role in China. The name Nanjing has become more popular over the last few decades, but Nanjing and Nanking are used interchangeably. The difference is mostly based on how the Chinese characters translate into Western letters. For the sake of consistency, this book will use Nanjing; however, if you are interested in learning more, Nanking tends to be used more often in historical context based on Western interpretation. Nanjing is the standardized version adapted during the 1950s as the preferred Eastern spelling.

Chapter 3 – Japan's Invasion of China

The start of the Second Sino-Japanese War was very similar to how tensions across Europe were built. Germany was able to acquire control over other nations through increasingly hostile tactics. The way Japan began to take over portions of Asia was similar because it initially started by stating claims over regions with largely questionable rights. By 1937, all pretense of a civil acquisition was gone, as Japan had become openly hostile, invading nations without any rights to their land.

Japanese Control of Manchuria

Japan had been exercising control over Manchuria due to its dubious claim over the region from the Twenty-One Demands. When Europe failed to restore the region to China, the country found itself in a poor position to try to reclaim Manchuria. With the Republic of China still working to form a government and with different divisions fighting for power, Japan was able to gain a much better foothold on the continent.

In 1931, Japan began to move farther into the region. On September 18th, they created an incident at the South Manchurian Railway to justify moving into Manchuria and occupying it, a move that was against the treaty they had signed with China. When part of the railroad was destroyed in an explosion, the Japanese declared it was an attack by the Chinese, pointing to the local garrison as the perpetrators of the explosion. Japan quickly moved into the area. The local government refused to fight, essentially letting the Japanese take control over a large portion of the province.

The leaders of China were unable to send anyone to fight the Japanese, so they turned to the League of Nations in the hopes that it would help. The harshest thing that the League of Nations did was to demand that the Japanese withdraw from the area by November 16th, 1931. Japan, particularly its military, dismissed this resolution. The League of Nations had no follow-up measures against the Japanese when they refused to leave. The US did pass the Stimson Doctrine, which said that the country would not recognize Japan's claim since it ignored China's sovereignty in the region.

With little action to actually dissuade them, the Japanese established their own puppet government over the region, which they renamed Manchukuo. At the head of the government was Puyi, the last emperor of China. Though this gave the appearance of legitimacy, the League of Nations quickly took the same stance as the US and refused to acknowledge the puppet government. With so many seeming to turn on them, Japan left the League of Nations in March 1933, a move that Germany would mirror that October. With the failure of the League to act to save members of its own organization from others within it, this was the beginning of the end for the organization. As remaining members lost faith in its ability, the League of Nations stopped playing any role in securing its member nations, and it finally dissolved in 1946.

Though Hitler was rising to power in Germany and the European nations were becoming increasingly aggressive, it was Japan's actions in Manchuria that would start the chain of events that would ultimately lead to the dissolution of many of the measures put in place after World War I. Before the next major movements in China took place, Japan, Italy, Spain, and Germany formed their own pact since they no longer belonged to the League of Nations.

During the Japanese occupation of Nanjing, many of the atrocities were committed on the Chinese people. However, with Japan controlling the narrative and the region and with no one to talk about the horrors, there is less documentation and stories about how the Manchurians were treated.

Start of the Second Sino-Japanese War: The Marco Polo Bridge Incident

It took a few years before Japan would act again. Their move to take over Manchuria had not resulted in any real action against them, but other nations were displeased. By biding their time, the Japanese were able to build up more forces on the continent. By 1937, the military had finished their preparations, so Japan began to move on to other regions, including Beijing, Shanghai, and eventually Nanjing.

Following so much unrest and this thinly veiled power grab in the name of expanding their empire, the Japanese ceased hiding their intent in 1937. Japanese soldiers were conducting exercises about thirty miles from Beijing, but they had not notified the Chinese, something that had traditionally been done to establish intent and prevent war. The exercises were taking place near the Marco Polo Bridge. When it was over, the

Japanese claimed that they had lost a soldier, and in return, they demanded that the Chinese soldiers allow them to enter Wanping, a nearby town, to look for him. When the Chinese refused to let them into their territory, the Japanese began to force their way to the town. Both nations reacted by sending troops to bolster their numbers.

The exercise startled the Chinese troopers who were stationed close to the training exercises, which resulted in a brief skirmish. Initially, Japan was able to take control of the bridge, but that was short-lived. At the end of the day on July 8th, only four of the one hundred estimated Chinese defenders survived the attacks of the Imperial Army. Japan controlled the bridge until the next morning when Chinese reinforcements arrived and reclaimed it.

The next morning, the tension built until the two sides began fighting at the bridge. The Chinese quickly took control, forcing the Japanese to pull back, and they established a short-lived verbal agreement. According to that agreement, China would issue an apology for what had happened, but military leaders on both sides would be punished for the incident. China would also replace the military troops with civilians who belonged to the Peace Preservation Corps. Japan was to pull back from the area. The agreement was signed on July 11th.

This minor incident seemed to have been easily resolved, but the way it was portrayed back in Japan would cause tensions to escalate. The Japanese Cabinet held a press conference and appeared to reassure the people that things were fine by announcing that both sides had reached an agreement. However, they also announced that they were mobilizing three new divisions in their army and issued a warning to the governing body in Nanjing that it should refrain from interfering with the solution that both sides had reached. Given that Japan was mobilizing to the region, Nanjing responded by sending out four divisions. With both sides clearly breaking the agreement, hostilities quickly began. On July 20th, Japan attacked Wanping, shelling the city, and by the end of the month, the Imperial Army had surrounded both Beijing and Tianjin. With two important cities under their control, Japan turned its eyes to the historically significant capital city of Nanjing. However, it was the assassination of one of Japan's naval officers at the beginning of August 1937 that would finally lead to the declaration of war. At the time, it was called the Second Sino-Japanese War, as Europe was still maintaining a delicate peace. However, it wouldn't be long before Japan and Germany would make their interests very clear as they took over nations around them.

Sanko-Sakusen: Planning to Invade Nanjing and the Three Alls Policy

Like the Nazis, the Japanese had a slogan that helped to dictate their actions during the war: Sanko-Sakusen. However, the Japanese did not create concentration camps and then put the motto over the camps' gates (most German concentration camps "welcomed" the prisoners with the slogan *Arbeit Macht Frei*, which translates to "Work Sets You Free."). Instead, the Japanese military followed a policy described as the "Three Alls": "Kill all. Burn all. Loot all." In the West, this is comparable to scorched earth tactics, which would be executed by the Soviets later in World War II as they retreated from the Germans. However, the Soviets were not trying to take over lands but rather destroy all potential resources, leaving the Germans with nothing to take but scorched earth. It was incredibly effective against the Germans, as it eventually meant they had to stretch their supply lines too long and too thin. Unfortunately, it was equally effective when used by the Japanese, but it also meant the slaughter of hundreds of thousands to millions of civilians wherever the Imperial Army went.

Japan would establish concentration camps, even creating a place that has come to be known as China's Auschwitz. However, the Japanese government didn't send people to a single location the way the Nazis did. More often, they would simply slaughter people where they lived. Ironically, when Japan took control of Manchuria, the Japanese wanted to populate the region with Jewish people fleeing from Europe, giving refuge to the people that Japan's allies were trying to exterminate. The area already had a large European Jewish population because many Hebrews had fled from Russia in the middle of the previous century. Japan helped Jewish people flee across Russia to settle in Japanese-controlled lands, and many saw this as a humanitarian project. Japan did stand to benefit, especially as there were many engineers, bankers, and other well-educated people looking for sanctuary. Still, it was clearly an affront to one of Japan's few political allies. The Japanese also did not seem to think of the Jewish refugees as equals. The plan to settle them was known as the Fugu Plan because they saw the Jewish refugees as being similar to pufferfish (known as fugu in Japanese): they are delightful when handled right but toxic if handled wrong.

The term Sanko-Sakusen was used by Japanese soldiers who discussed their actions nearly two decades later in 1957. They admitted to committing atrocities and acknowledged the ideologies behind their own horrific actions. Many of them pointed to indoctrination, which had children learning to idolize the emperor and military, resulting in obedience in doing what they were told. The idea that people of other nations were lesser made many Japanese soldiers look at the civilians more as objects than people, which allowed them to commit horrific acts without feeling regret. It would be a similar sentiment expressed by the Germans, although they primarily said that they simply didn't question orders because most of Europe no longer had the same sense of a beloved monarch or emperor by the 1930s and 1940s.

Over the first six months of the Second Sino-Japanese War, Japan had taken control of Tianjin, Beijing, and Shanghai. The Chinese people who survived told of the atrocities that had been committed up to the Imperial Army's arrival, though most of the atrocities were focused on quashing the Chinese as quickly as possible. Since these areas had a larger Western population (cities in port areas often had larger populations of Western citizens for business reasons, as well as members of the military to protect areas under the control of Western nations), the Japanese seemed to be more measured in their approach to dealing with citizens and prisoners of war. As Chinese leaders saw their land and port cities begin to be taken by the invaders, they did not ignore the warning signs. Knowing that Japan would move on Nanjing, China was faced with making a decision about how to react. With little time to make their move, the Chinese would make the only move they felt they could.

Chapter 4 – The Second Battle of Shanghai and Building Frustration and Resentment toward the Chinese

Between 1931 and 1937, China remained divided as the Nationalist Party and the Chinese Communist Party fought for control over the country. Even as anti-Japanese sentiment grew in the country, neither side was willing to stop their internal struggle until the Japanese began to take control of some of their most important cities in 1937. Following the slaughter at Shanghai, the Chinese would look for ways to save the people in their capital city as the Japanese turned their attention south.

No Good Options

Though China had been able to modernize, in large part because of the help it had received from Germany over the years since the end of World War I, the nation had been fighting a civil war for years by 1937. They knew that they could not beat the Japanese as they began to march farther into China. The two sides trying to run the government began to consider what they could do, knowing that they didn't have many good options available.

With the Japanese pouring in from their island and the other lands they controlled, particularly Manchuria, China decided its best option was to pull its resources and as many people as possible from the coastal area and move them away from the cities in the eastern part of the country. Just like Russia would do several years later, China would eventually adopt a scorched earth policy, destroying any potential resources that the Japanese might be able to use. This would be just as effective a method against the Japanese, who lived on an island that lacked those resources, as it would be against the Germans, who didn't have the proper resources and supplies for the harsh Russian winters.

In 1937, the Chinese began to move whatever they could from the cities, but the speed with which the Japanese attacked would make it difficult to make any substantial progress. At this time, the Chinese did not know the kinds of horrors that the Japanese would enact, nor would they adapt the scorched earth policy until they lost their important eastern cities.

Attack on Shanghai

After their success in taking over Manchuria in 1932, the Japanese attacked Shanghai. The Chinese had fought hard, losing many soldiers to the attack, but they had the verbal support of most of Europe (including Great Britain, which still kept troops in the area) and the US. Japan continued to send troops to the region, finally building a force of more than 100,000 men by the end of February 1932. They were about to defeat the Chinese forces in the areas around the city, but their victory was short-lived, as the Chinese forces in the city pushed back the invaders. The Imperial forces continued to attack at the beginning of March, and even though the Chinese forces that remained in the area were considered elite (the 87th and 88th Divisions had been trained by the Germans), they could not withstand the continued attacks by Japan. Europe and the US played small roles, but they helped to work out a ceasefire, giving Japan control over much of the area. This further angered the Chinese, but there was little they could do. This came to be known as the First Battle of Shanghai, and it set the stage for a much larger war just a few years later.

In 1937, the Japanese had established a much better foothold in the region, and they would soon begin the major initiative of the Second Sino-Japanese War. Up to this point, the fights had been on a much smaller scale. However, the Second Battle of Shanghai, also known as the Battle of Songhu, would make it impossible to restore peace.

The tension that had been building since 1932 reached a peak on August 9th, 1937, when First Lieutenant Isao Oyama tried to enter Shanghai's Hungchiao Airport, which was a breach of the signed agreement. The Chinese opened fire on him, killing the Japanese soldier. While apologizing for their officer's actions, the Japanese demanded the disarmament of the Chinese Peace Preservation Corps. When Japanese soldiers arrived in Shanghai to see to this disarmament, the Chinese refused. Based on the previous actions of the Japanese, the Chinese likely suspected that the disarmament was a precursor to war. If the Chinese soldiers were disarmed, they would then be much easier for the Japanese soldiers to defeat. Since it was their soldier who had been in the wrong, as he had broken the agreement, it made no sense for the Chinese to be the ones to disarm. Small clashes occurred in the city, and the Japanese troops requested reinforcements. When the Chinese military leader in Shanghai, General Zhang Zhizhong, learned of the Japanese request, he also asked that reinforcements be sent to support his troops.

Western leaders attempted to cool these tensions because open war would harm their interests in the area. Some nations had control over small areas in the region, while others had significant commercial and industrial interests that would be disrupted if the two strongest Asian powers were unable to come to peaceful terms.

The Japanese soldiers made their move on August 13th at nine in the morning by marching ten thousand troops into the Shanghai suburbs. The Chinese troops began attacking the invaders by the afternoon. The invaders, who launched airstrikes and sent in additional troops against the Chinese fighters, hoped to be able to finish the fight in about three days. General Zhang Zhizhong was able to drag the fight out to about three months. Unfortunately, the Chinese forces were simply unable to repel the Japanese. What Zhang had done was to allow time for some of the Chinese citizens to escape and to remove as many resources from the city as possible. Since the fighting occurred around three strategic areas (within the downtown area, in the towns around the city, and along the Jiangsu coast), the Japanese were unable to focus their attacks on one area, making it so the Japanese could not prevent the flow of people and industries from the city. With the fight going on longer than they had expected and with Japanese troops executing actions that their officers considered dishonorable (including many of the actions that the soldiers would take in Nanjing after it had fallen, just on a much smaller scale) to finish the fight as fast as possible, the Japanese felt a significant blow to their morale. The heavy loss of troops further demoralized the Japanese, but they ultimately won. After fighting in and around Shanghai for seventy-five days, the Chinese began to withdraw from the downtown area. The best fighters remained behind to hold off the Japanese, and the Chinese lost roughly 60 percent of those men. Initially, they had hoped for reinforcements, but they never arrived. However, the elite forces did help to ensure that the Chinese were able to prevent the Japanese from making use of their resources from the city. They also slowed down the timeline for Japan to begin their push farther south to Nanjing.

It is estimated that roughly 300,000 Chinese lost their lives during the battle, compared to the roughly 40,000 Japanese soldiers who died. It is likely that this serious loss of life significantly affected how the two sides viewed each other. Some think this could have contributed to the animosity and cruelty that followed the battle. However, given the medical facilities that were created to experiment on the Chinese soldiers (facilities that rival the human experiments of the Nazis) and the Three Alls Policy, the Japanese would have enacted atrocities even if they had managed to take the city in the planned timeframe.

The Western Witnesses of the Battle

Shanghai had been difficult to take in part because Western nations had created their own little havens within the city. There was a region in the city called the International Settlement. Shanghai was the second-largest Asian city (Tokyo was the largest), and it was a port for nations that had territories in Asia. When the Japanese attacked, Western citizens and military personnel witnessed the fight. They largely remained neutral as the two Asian nations fought for control of the city and surrounding areas. Ironically, the Japanese were one of the largest populations of civilians in the International Settlement. This could have helped contribute to the reluctance by Western nations to react, as they had largely seen the Japanese in a very different light outside of their military aspirations.

However, when the Japanese attacked civilians, some of the Western soldiers intervened, most notably working to help Chinese civilians who were trapped to get away from the invaders. However, they never directly fought the Japanese and largely left the Chinese to their fate. Considering how much difficulty they were having back on the continent, it is likely that the Westerners were attempting to avoid dividing their forces across two continents. They did see firsthand just how brutal the Japanese soldiers could be, but their presence likely kept the Japanese from committing the same kinds of atrocities they would in Nanjing.

A Hint of the Horrors to Come

When it was clear that the Chinese were either retreating or surrendering, the Japanese were merciless toward the soldiers they captured. Many of the Chinese soldiers who were still in the city went into the International Settlement to surrender instead of giving themselves up to the Japanese. Outside of the city, the invaders began to show how they were going to operate for the next few months. Even those who remained in the city weren't safe.

To help boost the soldiers' spirits, the Japanese troops forced many of the women who were still in the city to become "comfort women," essentially forcing them into sexual slavery. This was not the first time they had done that either; Chinese women in Manchuria had been forced to provide whatever the Japanese soldiers had wanted after the takeover roughly five years earlier. The practice was established after the Manchurian Incident at the request of military authorities, and as a result, brothels were opened to entertain men stationed in the region. The establishment of these brothels was documented, giving historians a better look at how the practice of comfort women began. The practice had been introduced in Shanghai after the first battle, with the first official station being made at the naval brigade near the city. At the time, it was thought that the establishment of these kinds of facilities would keep the soldiers from raping Chinese women in the area, which would build resentment of the Japanese. It was also meant to help reduce the spread of sexually transmitted diseases, as there was control over the women who were "comforting" the soldiers. This means that by the Second Battle of Shanghai, there were already brothels for the soldiers. However, at the beginning of 1938, when the leaders in Shanghai requested three thousand Japanese women to come "serve" the Imperial Army, perception in Japan shifted. The people accused the military of abducting women and tarnishing the public image and honor of the soldiers, so the use of Japanese women in the brothels dwindled. As there were regulations on which women could be brought from Japan in the early part of 1938, the military forced women from other nations into the brothels, including from Korea and Taiwan. While the war began before these regulations were established, opinion back in Japan had already turned, so the military had likely found other ways to ensure that their men were "comforted" with a lot less scrutiny from the citizens back home.

The Second Battle of Shanghai finally ended in the middle of November. By November 19th, the Japanese were pushing to keep the Chinese on the run, and they planned to force their adversaries toward Nanjing. Lieutenant General Yanagawa Heisuke had been the one to send word back to the Imperial Headquarters to begin the move south, but the military leaders appointed General Matsui Iwane to be the commander-in-chief. When Matsui fell ill, the emperor's uncle, Lieutenant General Prince Asaka Yasuhiko, became the commander of the force.

The events at Shanghai were actually similar to what was to come, both in Asia and in Europe. Historians often correlate the battles in Asia with the battles in Europe. For instance, the Second Battle of Shanghai has been called the Asian Stalingrad. One of the main differences was that most of the primary players in the war were present in Asia for the first major battle of what would become World War II.

Chapter 5 – War Crimes Committed on the Way to Nanjing

The Nanjing Massacre is often discussed, and it covered a period of about six weeks, but the atrocities that were committed by the Imperial Army began before they even left Shanghai. As the soldiers moved between the port city to the capital, they released their anger, aggression, and feeling of superiority on the people they encountered. Japanese journalists were often embedded within the military to relay information about how impressive the military was and how easily they crushed their enemies. One of these reporters recorded his impressions at the time, saying that the reason they were able to move so quickly was that they were able to do whatever they wanted along the way. They raped women they encountered and looted settlements. This was condoned, and some have reported it was even encouraged by many of those in charge.

Several books have been written about the period between the attack on Shanghai and the events of Nanjing because it is often overlooked. While the death toll was not as high during this time, the Japanese showed no mercy during the march.

Stories of a Callous Competition

One story that arose during this time revolved around a competition between two officers. According to the story, the two officers strove to see who could kill one hundred people the fastest using just a sword. Journalists sent stories back about the competition, likely as a way to help build support for the military. However, there is a question about how true this story actually was. The way that the alleged events were covered was more of a sporting event. Since the count was for one hundred men, it was not a competition that could be completed within a day. This meant that there was a daily account of these events as the men worked to get to the designated number of kills. Given what would happen in Nanjing, there are many people who believe that these accounts were true, that two men really did try to see who the most efficient killer was. However, there has been a lot of debate and doubt cast on the stories reported back to the Japanese citizens. Those who don't believe that the stories were real have argued that it was likely reporters were working to build pride in the military and heighten support. According to this theory, it was the soldiers who made up all of the stories. It would likely have helped to build their morale after the difficulties in Shanghai.

With many people having fled from Shanghai to Nanjing, many of the people who lived between the two cities likely fled as well. It would have been very obvious where the Imperial Army would go after their success in the major port city. Word of how the Japanese had treated the Chinese in and around Shanghai would likely have made it difficult to find many remaining Chinese people along the route, though not all of them would have the ability to flee. After all, the way many of the more rural Chinese were treated during the civil war was atrocious. There were reports of the Chinese leaders forcing their citizens into slave labor in some regions, particularly near the port cities. While many of the people between Shanghai and Nanjing weren't subjected to forced labor, they likely would not have had the money to leave. It is difficult to know how many people lived between the two cities because census information is not available.

The authenticity of the news reports about this particular competition is uncertain, but the details definitely originated within the military, even if it was just the soldiers coming up with tales to try to raise support back home. This showed a callousness toward the Chinese, especially if such tales would boost morale. It also helped to cement the frame of mind the soldiers were in when they headed toward Nanjing. The fact that they could so easily dispatch people and see it as a competition (whether or not it happened) indicates how the idea of the warrior was translated to then modern-day settings.

The Warrior Code and Indoctrination

For a long stretch of Japanese history, samurai were an honorable class and were considered among the elite, both in the military and in daily life. By the early part of the 20th century, the class of samurai had changed, and they largely helped to control the direction of the nation, particularly the growth and rapid expansion of the military. The idea of creating a Japanese empire appealed to the former samurai class. However, the change in weaponry made it easier to enlist a much wider group of soldiers. Lower social classes had always been a part of the military, but now, the leaders had much larger groups under their control. Though the samurai class was no longer a part of Japanese society, there was still a lot of respect for their actions, and soldiers bought swords that were either antique or similar to samurai swords. These swords were taken into battle so that soldiers would be able to commit suicide instead of being dishonored by defeat.

The need to fight for the emperor was impressed upon the citizens, and boys were able to enlist when they were just fourteen years old. While it was said that they fought for the emperor, it was largely the military that pulled the strings. By bringing such young boys into fighting, they were able to more completely indoctrinate them, something that many have compared to brainwashing. Death was considered to be the most honorable end, and this ideology was mixed with the older way of the warrior, a code for how samurai were to behave that was called Bushido. Some of the most extreme practices under this code included seppuku (committing suicide to atone for a failure or loss) and kamikaze (largely practiced by pilots who sacrificed themselves to kill as many of their enemies as possible). However, many other components of that code were ignored during the march between Shanghai and Nanjing. Bushido requires that a warrior be courageous, practice self-denial, and be loyal to their lord (during the 1930s, this had become the emperor).

Some have pointed to this code and how it was used during the 1930s and 1940s to indicate the soldiers' states of mind, but the comparison between the code and the actions of the soldiers at this time were significantly different. This is more obvious when going over the documentation of the events and how fervently some Japanese have denied that they even happened.

The mindset of the men by the time they reached the city was likely one of extreme patriotism and a desire to prove themselves. Due to ideas of being superior to the people around them, a negative view of women from other nations, and the idea that they were trying to prove themselves, the Japanese soldiers were in a mindset that likely contributed to the events that began once the soldiers entered the city as victors. It would not take them nearly as long to defeat the Chinese soldiers in Nanjing as it did in Shanghai, in large part because the Chinese had already evacuated all of their important figures. Citizens who could not afford to move and lower-level soldiers were left behind to face the invaders who had become agitated as they marched toward Nanjing.

Chapter 6 – The Order to Kill

The orders that were given are not entirely known because many of the accounts were given when the Japanese were put on trial for war crimes years after the war ended. The accounts given were varied, which could indicate the different experiences of the soldiers. Three men controlled large troops of men, and they each advanced on the city from different directions. General Matsui Iwane had been appointed the commander general, and he led an amphibious group. Nakajima Kesago was the leader of a large group of men who moved along the southern banks of the famous Yangtze River; this group came from the west. Lieutenant General Yanagawa Heisuke was responsible for the third group, which moved toward the city from the southeast.

Each of these leaders had a different approach to the war, and they likely inspired very different emotions from their soldiers.

- General Matsui Iwane was responsible for the attack on the city, and he was a well-respected leader within the military. He was a firm Buddhist and came from a family of scholars, and he seemed to try to live by these principles prior to the war. He had retired from the military but was called up to fight in August 1937.
- Nakajima Kesago has been described as cruel and violent. He was known for his specializations in intimidation, manipulation, thought control, and torture.
- Lieutenant General Yanagawa Heisuke was more like the stereotypical leader, and he valued discipline and liked to keep firm control over his troops.

All three of them arrived outside of Nanjing by the beginning of December. General Matsui Iwane had fallen ill by December 7th, 1937, and his replacement took over for him. As a member of the royal family, Asaka Yasuhiko had a lot more control over the men, as they would have wanted to serve him as a stand-in for the emperor. It was as if the crown had stepped in to lead them from the front lines. However, there were still two other men leading their own divisions into the city.

The commanders in Tokyo had sent the orders for the Imperial Army to occupy Nanjing on December 1st, but the men were not yet in place when the orders arrived. Matsui Iwane's health likely further delayed the plans. However, the orders were clear regardless of who was leading the troops. The Japanese had two objectives during this period:

- Take control of Beijing and establish another puppet government.
- Occupy Nanjing.

The attack on Shanghai had taken far longer than expected, so General Matsui Iwane knew how vital it was that the next major campaign did not take nearly so long to complete. With the Three Alls Policy in place, the troops had their orders to ensure that the campaign did not suffer any more delays. This was likely a contributing factor in Matsui allowing someone else to take over for the men under his command. However, before this happened, he impressed upon the men how important it was that they move swiftly and decisively. They were to represent the honor of Japan and should conduct themselves accordingly. However, it was also vital that they show how superior the Japanese were to ensure that no one else would want to face them again. He further reminded them that foreigners were to be avoided since they were not a part of the fight; they were also to "protect and patronize" any Chinese officials and citizens they encountered in the city. Matsui wanted to ensure that they avoided any misunderstandings. It is uncertain how things would have occurred if he had been the leader during the final assault on the city. It is unlikely that he would have been able to control the men enough to prevent the horrors that occurred, but he could have made an attempt to stop them. It is difficult to imagine he would have been able to prevent much of the atrocities, especially since he entered the city soon after it was captured, and the soldiers continued to inflict some of the worst treatment on civilians for over a month. They would even cease to recognize a neutral zone, inflicting the same treatment on foreigners.

Chapter 7 – Defending Against the Impossible

Before the Japanese arrived in Nanjing, the capital had an estimated population of over one million people. While the population had grown and shrunk over the centuries, since the summer of 1937, the city had seen a significant increase in the population because of the large number of Shanghai refugees. Nanjing had seemed like a safe location, but the Japanese quickly made it clear that they were going to head to the city, as it was crucial to China.

Attempted Resistance between the Cities

Soldiers who retreated from Shanghai made an effort to slow the Japanese, but they were vastly outnumbered and already tired from the fierce fighting in Shanghai. However, they attempted to stop the Japanese invaders several times during their retreat from the city.

One of the last times that the fleeing Chinese tried to stop, or at least slow, the advancing Japanese was to the east of Nanjing in the town of Kunshan. They were only able to slow the Japanese progress by a couple of days before the town fell under Japanese control. However, this did give people some time to flee, especially as the military likely would have had the occasion to tell them of the potential violence they faced when the Japanese took over Shanghai.

The soldiers managed to establish a defensive line between the cities, but the Japanese breached and destroyed it on November 19th. Seven days later, the Japanese overran the Xicheng Line. Though they had not been able to hold off the Japanese for long, it did buy the Chinese leadership more time to prepare defenses and make a strategy for how to protect Nanjing and its citizens.

The Chinese Power Struggle

One of the primary problems with Nanjing was Chinese politics and the power dynamic. There were two different thoughts on how they should defend the capital city. On one side, General Li Zongren believed that there was no point in attempting to defend the city and thought that the troops and resources were best used elsewhere. His plan was to declare the capital an open city, leaving the citizens vulnerable to an attack. Any troops in the area would be ordered to destroy resources, facilities, and goods that could be used by the Japanese. He didn't want the Imperial Army to be able to make use of the modernization that the Chinese had built up in their capital, and he was willing to completely lose the progress they had made over the decades to make it more difficult for the Japanese to move farther inland. Li Zongren thought by abandoning the city to the Japanese, Chinese troops and resources would be saved for a later confrontation when the Imperial Army would potentially be weaker. Two other important figures agreed with this plan: General Bai Chongxi and the German Army advisor, General Alexander von Falkenhausen.

However, Chiang Kai-shek was in charge of the effort, and he overruled all three of his subordinates. His concern was that simply deserting the city without even making an apparent attempt to save it would be detrimental to the nation's prestige on the international stage. He also said that such an obvious admission of their inability to fight the invaders would lower troop morale across China. He reportedly said, "I am personally in favor of defending Nanking to the death." Instead of agreeing to completely abandon the city, Chiang Kai-shek put General Tang Shengzhi in charge of 100,000 troops. The problem with the troops was that the majority of them were newly conscripted, so they were untrained. They would face Japanese forces that had recently finished a hard battle against well-trained Chinese troops in Shanghai, including a large number of elite fighters. The Chinese military personnel who were to fight for Nanjing did not stand a chance.

Tang knew that they didn't stand a chance as well, but he made a show of putting up an effort for a while. When he held a press conference on November 27th, 1937, he proudly announced that he and his men would stand and fight for China. At the same time, he warned the small population of Westerners who remained to leave because war in the city was imminent. The troops were sent to clear all of the trees and buildings within a mile of the city to prevent the Japanese from having anywhere to hide. This decision was considered very controversial, as it would mean that people fleeing from the Japanese would have to enter the city because there would be no shelter for them elsewhere. This would increase the population right before the Japanese attacked. And even if buildings were burned, they would still provide some shelter for the Japanese because the Chinese soldiers didn't have time to entirely demolish them.

Tang was fully aware that nothing he did would amount to much in the face of Japanese aggression, though. As he put on a stern front, he was attempting a couple of plans of his own. He agreed with General Li Zongren's proposition to declare Nanjing an open city. Tang seemed to put a lot of faith in the Westerners in the city because he went to them to help persuade the general that it was a mistake to fight. He also wanted them to help negotiate peace with Japan.

Though Tang tried, both plans failed, and he had to confront the Japanese with a large group of untrained men. It is unknown how many troops were active in Nanjing by the time the Japanese arrived, as some had fled prior to the invaders entering the city. However, they are thought to have outnumbered the Japanese troops.

Chapter 8– Nanjing's Disorganization and Failed Preparations

The Chinese soldiers and civilians fled Shanghai, but the Japanese soldiers were never far behind them since there was little delay between their success in Shanghai and their departure for Nanjing. The Chinese soldiers were too exhausted to put up much of a fight against the advancing soldiers, so they largely tried to slow the Japanese, with some of them surviving long enough to reach the capital city. The refugees and Chinese soldiers who headed to Nanjing found themselves again under attack by the Japanese, though it was nothing like Shanghai.

What the people in Nanjing did not know was that the military leaders knew just how hopeless the cause was. Chiang Kai-shek had made his decision to put up a front knowing that they could not win. His refusal to listen to his advisors would end up costing many of the people in the city everything.

The Questionable Preparations in Nanjing

Though the Chinese had managed to prolong the fight in Shanghai, the obvious superiority of the Japanese forces made it clear that it would be difficult to hold Nanjing.

After leaving General Tang Shengzhi in charge of Nanjing's defenses, Chiang Kai-shek sent most of the trained soldiers and government leaders from the city to set up Chongqing as a temporary capital. Chiang Kai-shek and his family left the city on December 7th to head for Chongqing.

Prior to fleeing from Nanjing, Chiang Kai-shek ordered that the citizens, including civilian government officials (only the members who were considered important to the nation), be forced to remain in the city so that they and the untrained soldiers could defend it. He went as far as to forbid the remaining soldiers from evacuating citizens. The soldiers also continued to destroy buildings, but this time inside the city.

With many of the refugees relaying the horrors of what had happened in Shanghai, many of the citizens refused to stay. Taking what they could, they left the city. However, hundreds of thousands of people remained in the city, including women, children, and elderly people. As the Japanese fighters neared, many citizens began to panic and fled the city in droves. Tang made another controversial decision and had all of the city exits closed to civilians to keep them from panicking, a decision that seems contradictory. He even burned boats that were on the Yangtze River to prevent people from leaving.

Though there were far fewer foreigners living in Nanjing than Shanghai, they did try to band together to ensure that the Japanese knew that they were a community of largely foreign businessmen and missionaries. They formed the International Committee, and they were headed by John Rabe, a German businessman. The committee worked to set up a neutral area where the Japanese and Chinese would have to refrain from fighting, and it would include a home for the civilians since they should not have been a part of the fighting. The established Safety Zone was roughly the size of Central Park (located in New York City, US), and they opened it in November 1937. Initially, they had only about a dozen refugee camps.

The Japanese arrived outside of the city on December 13th, 1937. It seems that word had already reached the people in the city that the Japanese were holding killing competitions and engaging in looting as they moved toward the city. Rumors spread that the Imperial Army was also leaving behind mass graves for those they had killed and that they were killing indiscriminately. Even though the number of Chinese soldiers was greater than the number of Japanese soldiers, their lack of substantial training and likely loss of morale (both from the desertion of their leaders and the news about the approaching army) made them a poor match for the invaders.

Comparison between Shanghai and Nanjing

If Shanghai had been a significant blow to the Japanese sense of pride, Nanjing would bolster their belief in their nation's superiority. The leadership in Shanghai had been cunning, making sure the Japanese divided their attention between different areas and forcing them to fight on several fronts. This was one of the reasons why they were able to shatter Japanese expectations that the war wouldn't take more than a few days. The Japanese had actually believed that they would be able to complete the entire war in three months, a belief that they had to reevaluate by the time they finally achieved a victory.

The Japanese military leaders were angry that they had been so wrong, and the soldiers had lost morale after the Chinese had proved that they would not be so easily defeated. However, the Japanese had faced one of the best Chinese military leaders, one who knew how to make the battle-hardy men who served him far more effective in the face of the enemy. The Imperial Army was looking for revenge and validation in their beliefs, so by the time they reached Nanjing, the soldiers were angry and ready to prove themselves. One soldier had lost his brother during the fights in the north, so when they reached Nanjing, he took out his anger about the loss by killing as many Chinese as he could. The Japanese military leaders had something particularly atrocious in mind to help harden their men, though they likely had not planned for what would happen over the first couple of months in Nanjing.

Perhaps they expected the same kind of fight that they had faced in Shanghai. It does not seem like they had any intelligence of what was happening within Nanjing beyond whatever discussions they were having with the International Committee that had created the Safety Zone. The foreigners who had established the Safety Zone had done so in a way that was similar to the one in Shanghai, so they made sure that the Japanese knew of it. The Chinese newspaper *Hankow Ta-kung-pao* had even reported on this zone, so people likely flocked to it as the Imperial Army neared. Since the leaders of the zone had let the Japanese embassy know, the embassy agreed that as long as no current or former Chinese soldiers or weapons were present, they would respect it. However, the Japanese did not provide any public support for the creation of it.

Since Tang would leave before the Japanese arrived, there was no real head of the Chinese military remaining in the city, which meant the soldiers did not stand a chance of defending it. They had months to prepare while the Second Battle of Shanghai was fought, but all of that time ended up being wasted because of the political turmoil within China. Chiang Kai-shek had no interest in protecting the city, and the remaining people in the city didn't have a strategy in how to face their enemies.

This was almost exactly what the Imperial Army had expected to face in Shanghai. And with 500,000 Imperial troops heading to the ill-prepared Nanjing, there was little that the Chinese could do.

Chapter 9 – Nanjing Falls

The attack began on December 9th, 1937, and by December 13th, the Japanese were marching into the city under the command of Prince Asaka Yasuhiko. It was the beginning of one of the worst atrocities of World War II, and the Imperial Army reveled in their quick and easy victory, especially after the difficulty they had in taking Shanghai. Over the next six weeks, the people who remained in Nanjing would face an army that was almost entirely without restraints. However, the events would not be without repercussions, as the Japanese had signed the Hague Conventions and had then gone on to ratify it. The actions of the soldiers would go directly against the agreement, and the blame for who was at fault would be one of the greatest points of contention later on.

The Retreat of the Chinese Soldiers

Japan had been sending in airstrikes against Nanjing since the beginning of December, further breaking the chain of command within the city. Outside of the city, the soldiers did not fare any better, leading to an incredibly quick defeat. With the poor coordination and lack of any real leader, the Chinese soldiers quickly realized they did not stand a chance against the invaders. Some still tried to fight, but soon, the majority of them were attempting to retreat. Knowing that they would be targeted by the invaders, many of them shed their uniforms and weapons, hoping that they would be able to blend in with the citizens.

Unfortunately, the officers had been quiet in their retreat and did not always pass on the information to their subordinates. Chinese soldiers who had not heard the order began to shoot at their own soldiers, believing that the men were deserting before the fighting even began. There were not many ways for them to retreat either, as the Japanese had nearly completely surrounded the city by that time. Some civilians also tried to flee, resulting in fewer people being able to get out of the city. After all, there was only one way for them to go, and many of them were crushed to death trying to get through the narrow gate. Some people died when they tried to climb down the walls of the city, while others drowned in the river, which was too cold for most people to swim in the winter months. The chaos going on within the city was of a very different nature than the fighting occurring outside it.

There were Japanese troops waiting along the river as well, so those who managed to get away from the city were at risk of being killed as the Japanese flotilla fired at them. Even the Chinese soldiers who made it out of the city really weren't prepared to fight the Japanese waiting outside of the walls. There was no counterattack planned.

Once it became clear that the Japanese had won, they demanded that the soldiers and citizens had to surrender or face the wrath of the Imperial Army. From a safe location outside of the city, Chiang Kai-shek refused to surrender, not wanting to look weak, especially after the events in Shanghai. Despite this refusal, he knew that the Chinese soldiers did not stand a chance, so he issued an order to the soldiers to begin evacuating the city. Unfortunately, it was too late for the people in Nanjing to leave since the Japanese were outside of the city waiting to enter.

The Hague and Geneva Conventions: Why the Citizens Should Have Been Safe

The Japanese reaction to the battle in and around Shanghai showed that they were not entirely restrained by the rules of war that had been established at the beginning of the century. However, the fact that they had been fighting in and around the city was likely used as an excuse for why their approach might have been considered justified. The Chinese fighters were fierce, giving the Japanese reason to feel that they were a real threat, even in a weakened state. Considering the ease with which the Imperial Army took Nanjing, it is possible the Chinese felt that the Imperial Army's actions wouldn't be nearly so brutal. After all, the resistance had been minimal, with most of it coming from the burning of the surrounding area prior to the Battle of Nanjing.

It is also possible that more citizens remained in the city because of the established rules around how armies were supposed to act. The expectations for how the invading army should act had been established by the Hague Conventions, which were held in 1899 and 1907 in the Netherlands. All of the world powers of the time had met to determine the way that soldiers who had been captured would be treated, as well as citizens that the military encountered. According to the agreement, it was illegal for any soldier or commander to commit war crimes. Japan was one of the nations that had signed on to the agreement, so they were bound by the established rules. The Hague Conventions even dictated the treatment of citizens and prisoners of war, prohibiting the mistreatment and killing of both groups. The Imperial Army had not followed the Hague

Conventions in Shanghai, but the events leading up to their entry into Nanjing were completely different.

The Hague Conventions primarily established that anyone who was either sick or wounded would be treated by their enemies as a neutral party. The laws dictating how prisoners were to be treated were also documented in the Geneva Convention of 1929. All prisoners were to be fed and treated humanely, something that was not universally practiced up to this point. While it was generally understood by most nations that prisoners should be treated well, there was no universal law ensuring that nations and soldiers who treated prisoners poorly would be held accountable in an international court of law. It further forbade things like hostage-taking, deportations, torture, and anything that would be considered "outrages upon personal dignity," including issuing a judicial sentence against people from other nations. It was under this convention that the execution of prisoners and civilians would be explicitly designated as illegal.

However, the prevailing ideology in the Imperial Army was similar to that of the Western idea of Manifest Destiny. The Japanese believed that China was destined to fall under their control, and this was based in part because of their belief that they were superior to the people on the mainland. For those in power in Japan, it was much more practical. As an island nation, Japan heavily relied on the agriculture and resources of the mainland, and by taking control of China, the island nation would have all of the resources it needed without having to negotiate for it. Japan had managed to modernize much faster than China, and it was also united. The people in the highest echelons of the government and military planned to treat China as a colony, and they had been instilling that mindset into their soldiers, not the rules and laws that they had agreed to during the Hague Conventions. The way the Imperial Army fought in

Shanghai wasn't just a result of their ferocity and the unexpected duration of the fight but was rather a result of the way the soldiers had been trained to think of their opponents. The march to Nanjing only intensified that belief as they killed and looted along the way, building up the idea that they were not only superior but invincible. It was the kind of mindset that ensured that they would ignore the conventions and enact some of the worst war crimes that the world had seen up to that point.

The City Surrounded

Though the Japanese were absolutely brutal up to this point, their actions were not illegal because the Chinese had not surrendered; they were simply fleeing. As one-sided as the fighting was, it wasn't technically illegal based on the Hague Conventions. The fact that the Japanese were an invading force likely would not have been held against them as they were following orders.

On December 12th, 1937, the Imperial Army stood outside of Nanjing, with the fighting all but over. There was no way for the Chinese soldiers or citizens to escape, and it is thought that tens of thousands of soldiers and more than 200,000 citizens were left behind to be at the mercy of the Imperial Army. The Safety Zone had a very small number of foreigners, largely Europeans and Americans, waiting to help where they could; some of the remaining people were medical professionals who hoped to help the wounded. The majority of foreigners left the city before the Japanese even arrived. There were also some Christian missionaries who remained.

On December 13th, Japan entered the city after an incredibly short fight. The Chinese citizens flocked to the Safety Zone, hoping that they would be protected in case the Imperial Army was as horrible as the rumors from Shanghai had portrayed them. They even allowed some Chinese soldiers to enter since the Japanese were so ruthless to the soldiers they encountered. One of their most important roles, though, was to serve as a neutral witness to the events that happened around them and report the atrocities back to their nations.

Commander Matsui's Commands

Though he was too sick to actually enter the city with the Imperial Army, Matsui Iwane wanted to ensure that his troops made it clear that the Japanese forces were impressive, both in terms of their abilities and their behavior. When he finally entered the city not long after the Japanese had taken over it, Matsui spoke in a way that was likely meant to be inspirational:

> I extend much sympathy to millions of innocent people in the Kiangsu and Chekiang districts, who suffered the evils of war. Now the flag of the Rising Sun is floating high over Nanking, and the Imperial Way is shining in the southern parts of the Yangtze River. The dawn of the renaissance of the East is on the verge of offering itself. On this occasion I hope for reconsideration of the situation by the 400 million people of China.

Nanjing had a long history of wars, invasions, and rebellions, but at this point in time, the city was already under a lot of strain. It had been the headquarters of the Chinese Nationalist Party. Though there was a desire to work together against the Japanese, there was also some underlying mistrust. There has been speculation that Tang Shengzhi did not have any particular loyalty to Chiang Kai-shek. This would work to Japan's advantage.

Matsui had come out of retirement to aid the military, so he would have been aware of the laws regarding citizens and prisoners, which was why he issued orders that forbade the Japanese soldiers from mistreating the Chinese people. The Imperial Army had already disobeyed this order in Shanghai, with the soldiers executing the majority of the Chinese fighters even after they had surrendered. They had also slaughtered male citizens in case those men were soldiers. They also began to steal from the surrounding area because they weren't properly supplied, particularly in regards to food. This meant that the citizens around Shanghai were left without supplies.

It is likely that Matsui hoped that his speech to the military would keep his men from enacting the same illegal behaviors in Nanjing. After all, there had been very little fighting to justify a harsh crackdown in the city. Unfortunately, the men did not listen to him.

When the Imperial Army entered the city, it was very different from their entry into Shanghai. They had only lost about one thousand soldiers, which seemed a very small price to pay in proving just how superior their army really was. They had not faced any significant fighting, and there were no big battles that actually proved their capability since the Chinese soldiers had been told to retreat before a more protracted fight could begin.

Chapter 10 – A Contest to Kill and the Execution of Chinese Prisoners of War

While the killing contest on the way to Nanjing likely is not entirely true or accurate, it did provide ideas for the Japanese soldiers. Before they had even entered the city, the Chinese soldiers in Nanjing had surrendered. According to the Hague Conventions, the soldiers who surrendered should have been taken as prisoners of war and been treated well by the Imperial Army. Instead, the Japanese soldiers would treat them as less than human.

Upon entering the city, the troops began to go through the city to round up all of the soldiers who had been unable to escape. They knew that some of the soldiers had exchanged their uniforms for civilian clothing. The Imperial Army entered homes and began to remove all men who seemed to be of draft age. The invaders even entered the Safety Zone to remove all men who could possibly be soldiers. While there were many soldiers who were rounded up, there was also a large number of men who were not affiliated with the Chinese military, including hospital employees, medical professionals, firemen, policemen, young teenagers, and others who had remained in the hopes that their lives would not be too significantly affected by the invaders. All of the men were treated as prisoners of war, regardless of if they were actually military or citizens. By December 26th, 1937, the Chinese were forced to register in the Safety Zone under the guise of ensuring that they weren't Chinese soldiers. Many of the soldiers had left the city by this time, leaving their families behind. The men between the ages of fifteen to forty-five who had remained were mostly civilians. Some of the Japanese officers had expressed the idea that it was "better ten innocents dead than an ex-soldier free," indicating just how little regard they had for their Chinese prisoners. It was also something that would help to later convict some of the Japanese officials, as this statement was completely contrary to international law.

Later, the Japanese soldiers seemed to try to make the argument that the fact that the plain-clothed soldiers were trying to hide was what made them dangerous. Considering that they had actually taken many civilians as their prisoners, not just soldiers, their argument did not hold up during the trials. Regardless of if they were soldiers or not, all of the prisoners had surrendered, meaning that they should have been treated according to the laws set forth in the Hague and Geneva Conventions.

After months of mounting resentment and a sense of superiority over the Chinese, the Japanese soldiers felt a need for vengeance against their opponents. Obviously, the need for vengeance was misplaced, as the soldiers in Nanjing had barely put up a fight. However, it was not the only reason why the Japanese took a much bleaker view of their prisoners.

They had been left to largely fend for themselves, finding food where they could since the three months they spent fighting in Shanghai. Knowing that they did not even have enough food to take care of their own military and knowing that the Chinese soldiers had burned a lot of the food in the surrounding area, it did not seem possible for the invaders to properly take care of their prisoners. Not only did they not have enough food, but they also lacked sufficient space for the large number of prisoners they had taken, particularly since they failed to differentiate between soldiers and male citizens. Then there was the potential threat that the Chinese soldiers posed, at least in the minds of the Japanese men. The Chinese force was still large, and by adding civilian men into the mix, there were a lot of prisoners that they had to control. There was the risk that the prisoners might cause them difficulties, so the Japanese began to look at them as a significant problem instead of viewing them as prisoners.

The Japanese planned to hold a parade to celebrate their triumph over Nanjing, and General Matsui Iwane was to lead the men on the victory march through the city. The invading force saw the prisoners as a potential threat or perhaps as an inconvenience, as soldiers would need to stay behind to watch them. Lacking training on how to handle prisoners and with no clear policy in place for the Imperial soldiers to follow, the Japanese commanders decided to set their own policy. Instead of trying to control the prisoners, the leaders ordered the soldiers to execute all prisoners, with no effort made to determine who was actually a soldier and who was a civilian. It is unlikely that most of the orders were made orally, but there is practically no written record of them except for some remaining records issued by lower officials. One of the orders that were received and issued on December 13th stated, "Execute all the prisoners in accordance with the Brigade's order. Regarding the method for execution, what about making groups of dozens each, tying them up, and shooting them one by one."[1] There was also no expressed method in how they were to commit the executions. The soldiers began to act in ways that were decidedly contrary to the way that Matsui would have seen as acceptable; to begin with, the order itself was against the established laws of war.

As a result, soldiers took it upon themselves to act in ways that were far crueler than simple executions. Perhaps inspired by the idea of the killing competition that they had discussed on the way to Nanjing, members of the Imperial Army began to follow through with the orders in whatever way they considered appropriate or entertaining. Some simply lined up their prisoners and executed them, similar to a firing squad. Others took to using their bayonets for a much more up-close and personal execution of their helpless prisoners. Some seemed to try to follow through with the idea of a competition, lining up between one hundred and two hundred men along the banks of the Yangtze River and then gunning them down with machine guns. Perhaps the most gruesome and cruel method of execution was conducted by the officers who had swords. These officers, who were supposed to control their own men, seemed more interested in showing just how brutal they could be, forcing prisoners to kneel before them before beheading them. There were reports of competitions among many of the soldiers to see who could kill the most prisoners, particularly as they tried to gun down as many as possible during one frenzied attack on the Chinese soldiers. Beheading was one of the most popular methods of brutal execution, but some Japanese soldiers used even more drastic and barbaric methods, including nailing their prisoners to trees, burning them alive, and hanging the prisoners by their tongues.

---

[1] Margolin, J-L. (2006). "Japanese Crimes in Nanjing, 1937-1938: A Reappraisal," *China Perspectives*, January/February 2006.

Many of the horrors that were conducted against the prisoners were actually captured by reporters and photographers. The documentation and images of the massacre of the defeated soldiers are still available, with some posted online as a reminder of just how horrific the experience was almost as soon as the Japanese soldiers arrived in the city (these images are difficult to look at due to the brutality depicted in them, so they have not been included in this book). It is likely that the soldiers did not know that their actions were illegal, but as the images show, what they did was clearly wrong. In the years following the end of World War II, soldiers would say that they were simply following the orders given to them. Some may have felt that their method of execution was acceptable because of how savagely the officers had attacked. The way they would recount the events of that first week is haunting, particularly as it was so similar to how soldiers in Nazi Germany were willing to follow their equally horrific orders.

By the end of that first week, an estimated forty thousand Chinese men had been murdered by the invaders. It was the first major war crime that would be committed over the course of World War II. Unfortunately, it was just the beginning of the horrors following the surrender of the city. The slaughter of soldiers and men who were at an age to be drafted was the start of a nightmare for the civilians who remained within the city. While the majority of the Chinese men were slaughtered in the first few days, those who were still alive would largely be killed before the Japanese commanders would regain control over their men.

Chapter 11 – The Rape of Tens of Thousands of People

As the Chinese prisoners were being executed outside of the city, the Japanese soldiers who remained inside the city walls began to commit atrocities against the citizens. Unlike the soldiers acting on orders outside of the city, the men who had entered Nanjing had no such orders to cause harm. Their actions would come to be classified as criminal acts, which means that the actions of these soldiers were not done in any military capacity. The soldiers have been said to have been undisciplined, but based on the barbarity of the attacks against unarmed citizens, the problem was not based on the soldiers' lack of discipline but indicated a much deeper problem.

The next three chapters examine the three primary types of crimes that the Japanese committed against the Chinese citizens who had no means of escaping Nanjing.

The first type of crime would come to be the inspiration for one of the names of the Nanjing Massacre: the Rape of Nanjing. For six weeks, the male Japanese soldiers moved around the city, doing whatever they pleased. A large number of them began to hunt women. They did not care how old a female was, with the age range for women and girls who were assaulted being between ten and sixty. The youngest known victim was only nine years old, while the oldest was in her seventies. Pregnant women were not safe either. Women were abducted and then raped by individuals or gang-raped by groups of soldiers who did not view them as people.

After being raped, many of the women were mutilated and killed, with children also falling victim to the barbaric actions of the invaders. Young children and infants who were considered in the way of soldiers who wanted to attack and rape their mothers or sisters were killed. Mothers and grandmothers who tried to prevent their younger generations from being taken were also killed.

While there were times when individual soldiers would act to rape women, more often than not, the invaders acted in small groups so that a woman would be assaulted repeatedly at one time and would likely face the same torture at a later date if they weren't brutally mutilated and killed after being gang-raped. These soldiers would eventually have to talk about what they had done, and they would say that they didn't want to kill the women after raping them but that they couldn't leave behind any evidence. During the war tribunals, soldiers generally had an easier time recounting the looting and killing they had committed, but they were visibly uncomfortable talking about what they had done to the women before killing them.

Women were raped in front of each other, and at times, they were raped in front of their families. Some of the women who were abducted were taken to where the Japanese soldiers lodged and would be held overnight or, in some cases, for more than a week, where they would be repeatedly assaulted as soldiers came and went. Those who were kept for longer periods of time were often forced to work for the soldiers, serving them and cleaning during the day, then being sexual slaves at night.

Women who resisted were attacked, often with the soldiers wielding bayonets. Sometimes resistance meant that their families would be attacked. Not all the women were murdered, likely because the soldiers knew that they would not have any further outlets for their urges if they killed all of them. It would take a while for a place to be established for comfort women, in large part because Nanjing would need to be safe before these women could be brought in. Since there wouldn't be an official establishment for those services, the women of Nanjing were sometimes forced into that position.

Over time, the Japanese soldiers even began to enter the designated Safety Zone to find women who had not already been raped and assaulted. The German leader, John Rabe, had one of the only effective ways to force the Japanese out of the zone without giving them a reason to attack. As the person in control of the Safety Zone, Rabe could stop them by showing the invaders his Nazi armband with the familiar swastika. The Japanese may have felt that they were superior to the Chinese, and it is quite likely that many of them felt that they were superior even to their allies, but the soldiers were not willing to risk getting into trouble for disobeying an easily recognizable ally. Even if the Japanese had not officially recognized the Safety Zone, a Nazi was in charge of the area, and he was clearly taking the role very seriously. Over the weeks of chaos, Rabe ended up taking up a position of protector, going around in his vehicle to help people in the Safety Zone from being assaulted. There are several stories of how he drove away soldiers who were raping women, once throwing a soldier off of a woman. There was another time when he startled another soldier so much that the man ran away without putting his pants on. His presence seemed to have caused the Japanese soldiers to fear being caught, a sentiment that the soldiers did not have for their own officers. This is an unfortunate illustration of how little the officers did to stop their own men. Other people in the zone would not have as much success in preventing the rape of Chinese citizens who were looking for refuge. This shows that there was a complete lack of respect for foreign nations, especially as people from within the Safety Zone began to send reports of Japanese behavior after they entered the city.

The raping, mutilation, and murder of women would last for much longer than the slaughter of the soldiers. Where most of the soldiers and young men were killed within a week, the women would be victimized for the six weeks the Japanese rampaged through Nanjing. It has been estimated that between 10 and 30 percent of women between the ages of fifteen and forty became sexual assault victims during this time. Some reports indicated that at the worst of the chaos, the soldiers were raping up to one thousand women a night. According to the Westerners who had stayed in the Safety Zone, they witnessed between eight thousand and twenty thousand incidents of rape, and there is no way to tell how many sexual assaults were actually perpetrated since there were no witnesses at times to report them.

The number of women who were raped is impossible to know because the soldiers did not keep records of this particular atrocity. There doesn't seem to have been any particular orders to address the problem either, with soldiers seeming to have been allowed to do as they pleased during the six weeks after they entered the city. However, there were witnesses to the barbaric treatment of the women, and it would mentally scar those who lived through the chaos.

Chapter 12 – Mass Killings and Desecration of the Dead

Almost as if to mirror the executions occurring outside of the city, the Japanese soldiers within the city seemed to want to relieve their aggressions in a similar way. They began to randomly stab citizens—women, children, and the elderly—with bayonets without warning. Some began to viciously attack and mutilate the citizens with knives, and the invaders seemed to be unconcerned as they ran over citizens with tanks as they made their way through the city.

Regular citizens were shot down in the streets when they tried to flee from angry soldiers. People who refused to give the Japanese what they wanted were killed. Reverend John Magee said of the invading soldiers that they "not only killed every prisoner they could find but also a vast number of ordinary citizens of all age[s]. Many of them were shot down like the hunting of rabbits in the streets. There are bodies all over the city." Some have described these killings as indiscriminate murders. While less was done to investigate the raping of women, the random slaughter of citizens was investigated almost immediately after order was restored to the city.

Over a six-week period, there were reports that some officers encouraged their men to be more inventive in how they killed the citizens. After several weeks of mindlessly killing many of the city's residents, bodies lay all over the city, and the roads were mixed with bodily fluids, precipitation, and fuel. The Japanese were aware that this was an ideal condition for numerous illnesses to fester, so they were forced to change how they continued to kill the people of Nanjing.

It seemed that all pretext of pretending to be concerned about soldiers was gone, and the Imperial soldiers began to round up citizens to kill them in locations that have since been described as slaughter pits. Whether or not they were actually directed to do so, the soldiers did start to become more creative and crueler in their methods of killing the people at their mercy. Some of the civilians were buried alive, while others became living practice dummies for soldiers, who practiced maneuvers with swords and bayonets. Other innocent civilians were covered in gasoline and burned alive, something that had been done to Chinese soldiers during the first week. The location where these unimaginably inhumane acts occurred was near the Yangtze River, so the soldiers threw their victims in the water to be taken from the city when they were done. Some have described the river as being so full of human bodies that it appeared to be red with their blood.

Initially, the Japanese seemed to try to properly take care of the bodies following the killings. Between December 24th, 1937, and January 6th, 1938, over 5,700 bodies were buried near the Hepingmen Gate, including both soldiers and civilians. Between January 6th and May 31st, 1938, nearly seven thousand bodies were buried elsewhere. The Japanese recorded that roughly fifty-seven thousand people were buried, but they did not have the manpower and money to continue to bury all of their victims. After some sort of order was restored, residents from the city would begin to bury some of the dead, and it is estimated that 260,000 were buried by the end. But not all the bodies were buried. Some were burned, others were left in the river, and others were used for target practice. The bodies of the victims were often treated with as little respect as the living Chinese civilians.

There is no record of just how many people were killed during this time. However, the body count should not be the focus of the atrocities; instead, what is important is the undeniable evidence of a large-scale massacre. Whole numbers can be debated, but there is simply too much evidence to ignore that war crimes had been committed by the Japanese. The methods of killing the Chinese outside the city showed that at least the execution of the prisoners of war was not a result of undisciplined soldiers doing whatever they wanted but of a complete disregard of international law by the officers. The executions were systematic and well organized, even if the methods were not uniform. There is little evidence of direct orders for most of the killings that occurred within the city, but with the raping and killing of civilians going on for weeks, it is impossible to ignore that the officials at least tolerated the behavior. All of this was clear to those who witnessed what was happening, and it would come back against the officers and those in command after the end of the war. Until that time, though, the leaders did little to bring their officers under control until the Japanese high command finally learned of the events and sent orders to stop the chaos within the city. Whatever the military leaders in Japan wanted, the massacre of the Chinese civilians certainly was not a part of their plan. They ultimately wanted to control China, which meant that they needed a workforce and buildings from which to rule.

For a month and a half, the city was a living nightmare for the people who resided there, and even after order was restored, they would have little hope that the Japanese would honor international law; after all, both the Chinese and the Westerners had seen how little the Japanese military and government controlled their invading force.

Chapter 13 – Stealing the Valuables and Destroying the City

As the Japanese soldiers made their way through the city, they began to steal from the citizens, often at gunpoint. Soon, they began entering homes, stealing what they could take with them when they left the city. As if trying to hide what they had done, they began to burn buildings and homes. They also vandalized Nanjing, further destroying the city after the bombings that had occurred prior to the Imperial Army's arrival.

During the chaotic reign of the soldiers, extensive looting and arson took place around the city, similar to what the Nazis would do in Jewish ghettos a few years later. The primary difference was that the Japanese were destroying older buildings, stores, and homes in a city with historical significance to the Chinese. This could have been a method to further demoralize the Chinese living in other cities.

While the soldiers did not destroy the buildings within the Safety Zone, they did steal from the refugees who were there. The invaders took food and what little possessions that the refugees had. There wasn't much the International Committee in the Safety Zone could do to stop the soldiers from what they did outside of the zone, and there were only a few actions they could take against soldiers in the Safety Zone, as the soldiers could turn against them as well. Given the horrors that the soldiers were committing around them, it is easy to see the dilemma that the International Committee and the Westerners faced. To keep any kind of protection for refugees, they couldn't do much of anything to intervene in what they were witnessing. Fortunately, many of the vital facilities were located within the Safety Zone, including medical facilities, administrative buildings, and educational buildings. This did mean that most of the structures that housed things of monetary value (such as art) were vulnerable to the soldiers.

Some of the looting was chaotic, but there were elements of it that were far more calculated and efficient. Trucks were brought in to take away larger objects, creating something akin to a convoy. These trucks quickly removed valuables from Nanjing, probably to ensure that the things didn't burn when they could help fund the army. This particular crime was not perpetrated only by the soldiers, as the officials also participated as well. The officers often had the first pick of what they wanted and looted the most valuable items. One of the more notorious officers, Lieutenant General Nakajima Kesago, responded to General Matsui Iwane (who was upset by the looting) by saying, "Why does the stealing of art pieces matter so much when we are stealing a country and human lives? Who would benefit from these items even if we left them behind?" As callous as this sounds, the lieutenant general did have a point. Matsui had failed to stop other crimes that were far worse; the theft of items was not nearly so important.

When most of the valuables were gone, the Japanese began to destroy the buildings that remained standing. The only area that seemed to be largely left alone was the Safety Zone. Nearly every other part of the city would be all but unlivable by the end of those first six weeks. It is estimated that as much as a third of Nanjing was demolished by looting and other acts of destruction. Shops and businesses were completely looted, so there would not be much for the Chinese to return to once something like normalcy was restored in Nanjing.

How much of this was ordered by Japanese officials is difficult to say, but it is obvious that they knew what the soldiers were doing around the city. The number of burning buildings without any active fighting would have been impossible to miss. It was probably permitted (if it wasn't ordered) because it would help to destroy Chinese culture within the city. With the deterioration of the ancient culture, it would be easier for the Japanese to come into the city and reshape it as they pleased. The Japanese did spend most of 1937 and 1938 trying to divide China into fragments that would be easier to control. It was only after facing a lot of resistance that the Japanese would stop trying to break up the nation (during 1939 and 1940) and simply strive to conquer the nation as it was.

Chapter 14 – Reports of the Rapes and Atrocities Reach the Generals and Investigations Begin

One of the greatest debates that have occurred since the horrific events in Nanjing was determining who was to blame and how high up the chain of command one needed to go to find the culprits.

The Accounting of the Events from the Nanjing Safety Zone

Though the Imperial Army did not entirely honor the Nanjing Safety Zone, many of the foreigners who lived there were left alone (although the Chinese citizens were not as lucky). The Safety Zone acted as a place of refuge for as many as 200,000 Chinese citizens, and the foreigners took in as many people as they could between the arrival of the Japanese and until the zone was dissolved in February.

The foreigners soon acted in an equally critical role when the Japanese soldiers began raping and killing citizens, something that they knew was against the laws of war established by the Hague Conventions.

Initially, the European and American citizens began to send reports to Japanese diplomats, hoping that they would intercede and stop the barbaric practices of their own soldiers. These letters include accounts of the things that the Westerners in the Safety Zone witnessed, which they had added to emphasize that the presence of foreigners was not enough to persuade the soldiers to act in accordance with the laws. The letters came to be known as the "Cases of Disorder," a name that doesn't accurately reflect the severity of the problems or the contents of those letters. As a result of the horrors, the International Committee within the Safety Zone began to record the events, perhaps in case the Japanese did not do anything to stop the raping and unchecked massacres or perhaps so that they could report back to their own nations to let them know how brutal the Japanese soldiers were. It is also possible that the people within the Safety Zone planned to use the information against the Japanese later on as proof that war crimes had been committed. One of the recorded accounts from the Cases of Disorder recalled some of the actions of the Japanese soldiers at a Chinese temple:

> Many Japanese soldiers arrived, round[ed] up all the young women, chose 10, and raped them in a room at the temple. Later the same day a very drunken Japanese soldier came into one room demanding wine and women. Wine was given, but no girls. Enraged, he started to shoot wildly, killing two young boys, then left.

This is just one of many harrowing accounts of how little regard the Japanese soldiers had for the people living within the city. Another

Westerner who wrote home about what had happened was Robert Wilson. He recounted the events he had witnessed, although it is uncertain why he would retell the events to his family as they were fairly traumatic.

> The slaughter of civilians is appalling. I could go on for pages telling of cases of rape and brutality almost beyond belief. Two bayoneted cases are the only survivors of seven street cleaners who were sitting in their headquarters when Japanese soldiers came in without warning or reason and killed five of their number and wounded the two that found their way to the hospital.
>
> - December 15, Robert Wilson
>
> They [Japanese soldiers] bayoneted one little boy, killing him, and I spent an hour and a half this morning patching up another little boy of eight who had five bayonet wounds including one that penetrated his stomach, a portion of omentum was outside the abdomen
>
> - December 19, Robert Wilson

Accounts like these recorded by the International Committee would later be used to help highlight just how out of control the invaders were in those early days and how slow the Japanese government and commanders were to bring the problem under control.

Ultimately, it was the letters and cases that the Westerners kept during those nightmarish six weeks that would become the record of what had happened. Many of these documents are still available. There are far fewer accounts from the victims themselves, though they likely had no one to ask for help. The officials had fled before the invaders had even arrived, leaving behind largely untrained soldiers and citizens to fend for themselves against an incredibly hostile and agitated enemy. Still, there are some accounts of what happened from the Chinese victims, and they are kept with the accounts written by the Westerners.

In another strange twist of irony, John Rabe wrote to Adolf Hitler, hoping that the Führer would intervene to save the Chinese citizens. It is a strange note of sympathy by a person who was a part of a party that would enact equally horrific atrocities in Europe. Both sides seemed able to recognize the atrocities of the other while failing to correlate the same condemnation for their own. It gave both sides a sense of superiority over the other while having the same inability to recognize how similar their ideologies were. Whatever was said in Rabe's pleas, Hitler chose to ignore the appeal for help. Along with his requests for help, Rabe kept his own diary of the events. This would eventually be made available for people to read at the end of the century, showing just what the people in the city experienced as the Japanese soldiers moved about unchecked and uncontrolled around the city.

The High Command's Reaction

As of February 5th, 1938, members of the International Committee had sent over 450 correspondences to the Japanese Embassy alone, detailing the behavior of the invading soldiers. Many of the activities of the soldiers within the city had not been committed based on orders from the Japanese high command, so the accounts from the Westerners were likely shocking. In addition, the reports were too numerous to ignore. Japan's military had tight control over the media narratives about what the troops were doing, and the events in Nanjing were definitely something they did not want the Japanese people to learn about, so they went to great lengths to cover up any records of what had happened, starting with the reports that were taken by those in the city.

Knowing full well just what kinds of atrocities their soldiers had committed in Nanjing, the military continued to portray the men as heroes so that the general Japanese population would continue to support the nation's drive to become an empire. They seemed to be following the traditional method used by every other nation that strove to be an empire, regardless of how successful those nations were in the long run.

The First Investigation Begins

In March 1938, an investigation into this obvious criminal activity began. It was headed by Lewis Smythe, an American Christian missionary and sociologist who had remained in the Safety Zone. With the assistance of approximately twenty students from Nanjing University, they began to collect data about the number of people killed during those chaotic weeks following Japan's victory.

They first went to Jiangning Xian, which was located outside of Nanjing, where they obtained some staggering statistics.

- Roughly 9,160 people were murdered in the region.
- Over three-quarters of those killed were men.
- Nearly 60 percent of the murdered male civilians were men between the ages of fifteen and forty-four, and they were likely killed under the guise of ensuring that they weren't soldiers.
- About 11 percent of the women killed were between fifteen and forty-four years old. This age group was also the most targeted for rape.
- About 83 percent of the women killed were over forty-five years old.
- Roughly 8 percent of those who were killed were children between the ages of five and fourteen, and about 2 percent were children who were four years old and younger.

These findings suggested that more older women remained behind, likely believing that they would be somewhat respected by the Imperial Army. These women probably were tasked with ensuring that their homes and stores were protected and that order would be restored as soon as possible. The rest of their families had either fled from the area or, especially if the Japanese were too close, headed to the Safety Zone. This would explain why there were fewer people in the region but a higher number of elderly women. Due to the number of older women killed, it is clear that the Japanese did not provide them any amount of respect. Some of the women were killed outright, while others were left in the buildings when the soldiers burned them to the ground.

Chapter 15 – Declaring the Restoration of Order

Ironically, the Japanese had started trying to get Chinese citizens to return to work during the early part of January 1938, even as the soldiers continued to rape, loot, and kill them. One of the reasons this was necessary was that the Japanese simply did not have the necessary supplies to feed themselves. They had managed to make off with a lot of valuables, but those objects wouldn't be worth anything if the Japanese did not survive the occupation of Nanjing. By the end of January, the Japanese soldiers had started forcing people who had taken refuge in the Safety Zone to return to their homes or whatever remained of their homes.

When alone with one of his assistants, General Matsui Iwane was said to have expressed his shock at how horribly out of control things had gotten:

I now realize that we have unknowingly wrought a most grievous effect on this city. When I think of the feelings and sentiments of many of my Chinese friends who have fled from Nanjing and of the future of the two countries, I cannot but feel depressed. I am very lonely and can never get in a mood to rejoice about this victory...I personally feel sorry for the tragedies to the people, but the Army must continue unless China repents. Now, in the winter, the season gives time to reflect. I offer my sympathy, with deep emotion, to a million innocent people.

- General Matsui (reported in Iris Chang's *The Rape of Nanking: The Forgotten Holocaust*, 1991)

General Matsui was aware of what was happening in the city, and several times, he issued orders to his men to "behave properly," something he had originally instructed them to do. However, these were not the kinds of well-trained soldiers that he had become accustomed to. The soldiers were younger and had been trained under a different ideology than what had been prevalent when General Matsui had initially served in the military. It is said that when he stood to address the Imperial Army in February 1938, he was holding back tears. As he upbraided the men who had behaved in a way that was contrary to what was honorable, he believed that the actions in Nanjing would do irreparable damage to the image that the Japanese military had tried to create. Perhaps he knew that there were simply too many witnesses for the crimes to be completely covered up. From the Westerners who had been there to witness it to the living victims, Matsui probably had enough experience in war to know that the damage done was on too large a scale for it to be swept under the rug. It was also likely that he was ashamed that he had not kept his men under control. Compared to the other two commanders and the prince, General Matsui had built his reputation on honor and respect. Nothing about what happened since the army arrived in China had met his expectations of how the Chinese should have been treated. It is also likely that he knew that Western nations would focus more on the events in Nanjing and find it to be proof that the Japanese had become modern only in regards to their economy. The actions of the military were barbaric and chaotic, something that would definitely taint Japan's reputation around the world.

The Safety Zone was dissolved in February 1938 as the Japanese began to establish a government for the city. As Japan tried to create some semblance of order, they began to recall the people who were responsible for keeping the men under control. Matsui and Prince Asaka Yasuhiko were both told to return to Japan, where General Matsui resumed his retirement from active military service. It is thought that he may have suffered from tuberculosis, and he had also shown that he was no longer able to keep control over men the way he had when he was younger. Though he was retired, the former general did act as a military advisor for the next two years, helping the Cabinet as they made decisions on how to proceed as they fought farther into China and began heading south toward the Philippines. In the early part of 1940, Matsui was actively helping to get a statue of Kannon (the Japanese deity of mercy and pets) made and placed in Atami, the town where he lived. When it was erected, the statue was turned to face the direction of Nanjing. Later in the war, he did travel some, going to Burma, China, Malaya, Thailand, and a few other places in his role as the president of the Greater Asia Association. For most of the rest of World War II, his role was more muted, though the former general did remain active over most of the time between 1938 and 1945.

Chapter 16 – Wang Ching-wei, the Puppet Government, and the End of the War

The upper echelons of the Japanese military and government knew that they needed to put someone in charge of the city who would help to quell the unrest that their soldiers had caused. Clearly, they could not put a Japanese citizen as the head of the Chinese city, so they found someone they felt they could control. The man they selected was Wang Ching-wei. By the time Wang died, the Japanese had much more significant problems, so the region was largely left to fend for itself.

A Brief History of Wang Ching-wei

Born in 1883, Wang had been raised as a student of traditional Chinese education. His family was a part of the minor gentry in China at a time when there was much political upheaval. He learned all of the important cultural arts, including calligraphy, poetry, and Chinese prose. This would help him become an adept orator as he grew up. He first seemed to take an interest in the government in 1903 when he successfully took the civil service exam. This earned him a scholarship that would take him to Japan, where he attended Tokyo Law College. During his time in Japan, he would become one of the founding members of the T'ung Meng Hui, an association that sought a revolution in China. Due to his amazing way with words, he became one of the major propagandists for the group. Wang gained attention as a national figure when he helped in the attempted assassination of the Chinese prince regent. When that failed, Wang was arrested for his role and was jailed between 1910 and 1911. During the 1911 Revolution, he became one of the primary negotiators between the two sides.

Wang married in 1912, then moved to France, where he continued his education until 1917. Upon his return to China, he resumed actively supporting Sun Yat-sen, the first president of the Republic of China. During this time, Wang distinguished himself, and that when Sun died in 1925, Wang became the head of the KMT (the Kuomintang Party) and the revolutionary government that they were forming. When Chiang Kai-shek led a military coup against the revolutionaries in 1926, Wang fled from the region. He would return the following year, soon becoming the leader of the Nationalists' Wuhan government. Initially, he and his party aligned with Chiang, but within a year, Wang found himself disagreeing with the Communists. As his views changed, the party forced Wang out of the leadership position that he had held in the party. He found a new position as the primary opponent of Chiang and his methods within the KMT, and he supported several attempts to oust Chiang from power until 1932.

Following the Manchurian Incident (when Japan managed to reoccupy the region in 1931), Wang and Chiang put aside their differences as they realized that there was a much bigger problem they had to face. The pair formed a coalition and worked to establish a policy of minimal resistance as the Japanese took over the region. Both Wang and Chiang knew that the Chinese military was not strong enough to face the Japanese, so they were hoping to buy some time to build and strengthen the army. Between 1931 and 1935, Wang served as the prime minister, working with his opponent until there was an assassination attempt on his life. The attempt was unsuccessful, but Wang was hurt, and the bullet remained in his body. Perhaps feeling that he was no longer able to serve in the capacity they needed, the party and Chiang forced Wang to retire.

As the Second Sino-Japanese War began, Chiang's control over the party would increase, while Wang's power would continually be diminished. Wang's forced retirement did not stop him from participating in politics and the party, and he was able to get another high position within the KMT. However, he became more of a symbol than a member with actual power. As he was no longer instrumental in the power dynamic, Wang would have a better vantage point to see how the Chinese were suffering under Chiang, as well as to hear rumors of how the Japanese were treating the Chinese people during 1937. It was said that he acted in a way that he thought would ease the suffering of the Chinese people, as well as in a way that was designed to weaken Chiang's power over the party. Wang wanted to establish a peace settlement with the Japanese to stop the violence.

Following the Rape of Nanjing and the other atrocities committed by the Japanese forces as they moved farther into China, Wang's ideas would be unacceptable. During December 1938, he would be forced to flee from China, finally settling temporarily in Hanoi. Since he had been trying to work with the Japanese prior to his departure from China, they decided to offer him a position to head a new regime in China. The Japanese leaders assured him that he would be autonomous, so Wang accepted the position.

Japan Loses Control as Germany Falls

Despite the assurances that he would be in control, Wang was little more than a puppet for the Japanese government. He was also very ineffective in his attempts to stop the fighting in his region. Wang held his position until 1944. That year, Wang tried to have the bullet removed from his body, and during the operation, he died, leaving the region with no puppet for the Japanese to control. However, by this point, the US had entered World War II. The young nation, angry about the attack on Pearl Harbor, was proving to require nearly all of the attention of the Imperial Army. Trying to control the regions of China was not as important as stopping the US from attacking Japan.

No matter how hard the Japanese fought, they had no path forward to win. They were stretched too thin and were trying to control regions where the Chinese had executed scorched earth policies, so they simply did not have access to the resources they needed to stand up to the US. They also could not rely on Germany. Hitler and his nation were clearly not going to win their fight in Europe. On May 8th, 1945, Germany unconditionally surrendered to the Allies. While most of Europe was destroyed by the war, the US had joined World War II late (they declared war on the Axis Powers in December 1941, following the Japanese attack on Pearl Harbor, Hawaii). Apart from the attack at Pearl Harbor, very little of the US had been affected by the war (Germany and Japan had tried to attack with balloons and submarines, but by 1945, both nations were too focused on protecting their own lands). The US was rich in resources, had a much larger population, and its military forces had not spent nearly so many years fighting. Japan had started the Second Sino-Japanese War in the summer of 1937, which means they had been fighting for over four years by the time the US joined. By 1945, the Japanese had been fighting for nearly a decade, while the US had only been engaged for four years.

In addition to having more resources and less weary soldiers, the US had something that the rest of the world did not know about: the first nuclear weapons. It was clear at the beginning of 1945 that Germany would soon fall, so British Prime Minister Winston Churchill, US President Franklin Delano Roosevelt, and Soviet Premier Joseph Stalin met in Yalta to discuss what to do with Germany and how to end the war in Asia. At the time, the US wasn't sure when the nuclear weapons would be functional, so when the group met in Yalta (in what's come to be known as the Yalta Conference) in February 1945, the UK and the US saw value in having the land support of the Soviet Union. The three national leaders discussed how the Soviets would attack Japan, even though Japan and the Soviet Union had established a peace agreement a few years earlier. If the Soviets provided military support against Japan, they would be given a lot of influence over Manchuria following the Japanese surrender. They also decided how they would divide up the nations that the Nazis had invaded, with the Soviets gaining a lot of influence over the eastern part of Europe and the UK and the US having more influence over the western part.

Roosevelt died soon thereafter, and Vice President Harry Truman became the president. The hope that the US and the USSR would be able to take a less adversarial role following the war was soon quashed, for Truman's administration conflicted with the Soviet leader. When Churchill was voted out of office and a new prime minister joined the three nations, Stalin was said to have refused to even recognize the new leader. The combative relationship between the countries became much more pronounced after Germany surrendered. Stalin still held up his end of the agreement, though, sending his men over to fight Japan. The US worked as quickly as possible to finish the bombs in the hope that they could force the Japanese to surrender before the Soviets engaged in fighting. If the Japanese surrendered first, the agreement from the Yalta Conference would not be valid, so the Soviets would not have as much say.

In addition to wanting to nullify the agreement with the Soviet Union, the US was also concerned with the number of lives that would be lost if the fighting continued. The Japanese were much stronger than the Germans were by 1945 (they did not face the same level of resistance that the Germans did), so estimates said that the war would go on for years. The atrocities that the Japanese had carried out in the regions that they controlled were fairly well known, so the loss of life would likely have been much greater. However, the US focused mostly on the loss of their own soldiers in their calculations. Ultimately, they decided if the atomic weapons could end the war faster, it was worth the loss of Japanese civilian lives.

In the early part of August 1945, the US dropped leaflets over several Japanese cities (a common practice used during World War II), warning the citizens that they were going to be bombed. This not only acted as a way to reduce morale, but it also pushed the citizens to pressure their government to surrender. In theory, it also gave them time to flee. This initial set of warning leaflets was called the "LeMay leaflets," and they were dropped over Hiroshima. The warning was pretty standard; however, there was no mention of a new bomb that would be worse than anything the people could imagine at the time. The second round of leaflets was dropped over several other cities, and the image included a mushroom cloud. However, the text discussed the coming Soviet invasion, which would start on August 9th, 1945. Records suggest that Nagasaki did not receive this leaflet until after the city had been almost completely destroyed.

As they warned the people, the US, the UK, and the USSR warned Japan to surrender before the end of July, something that Japan refused to do. Perhaps the Japanese could not yet recognize that their defeat was imminent, even without the use of nuclear weapons. However, they were the last remaining Axis Power, which means that all of their enemies were entirely focused on them. It wasn't a question of if but when they would lose.

On August 6th, 1945, just before 9 a.m. in Japan, a small group of US bombers flew over Hiroshima. All of them released bombs so that the pilot and crew would suffer from the same amount of guilt after the destruction of the city. The Americans may not have known exactly how destructive it would be, but they did anticipate that it would be worse than any of the previous aerial bombings. Later, it would become known that the crew of the *Enola Gay* was the aircraft that carried the live nuclear weapon nicknamed "Little Boy." The crew would later express pride in their efforts, not grief or guilt, something that seems more chilling now since the effects of the bomb have become well known.

The Japanese suddenly lost all contact with an entire city. They were again warned to surrender, but the military leaders were attempting to figure out what had happened. The US only gave them three days, which was not enough time for them to witness the devastation—it wasn't enough time for the Japanese to fully consider their options, as atomic weaponry was beyond most people's comprehension at the time.

On August 9th, 1945, just after 11 a.m. in Japan, the US dropped its second atomic weapon on the city of Nagasaki. One survivor, Reiko

Hada, who was only nine years old at the time of the bombing, relived the experience:

> A blazing light shot across my eyes. The colors were yellow, khaki, and orange, all mixed together. I didn't even have time to wonder what it was...In no time, everything went completely white. It felt as if I had been left all alone. The next moment there was a loud roar. Then I blacked out.

Japan gave its unconditional surrender on August 14th, 1945. The final surrender was signed on September 2nd, 1945. World War II was over, but the Cold War was about to start. The adversarial relationship between the US and Japan would quickly change as the relationship between the US and the USSR became more tense. The US knew it needed more allies in the East to prevent the further spread of communism in Asia.

With the end of World War II, the Chinese Civil War would resume, but whichever side won, the nation would be communist. That left just a few nations as potential allies for the US, including Japan. Unlike the nations in the West, where power and influence were largely divided between the UK, the USSR, France, and the US, Japan was under the near-complete control of the US (the regions Japan had occupied were restored to their respective countries, except for Manchuria, which was under the influence of the USSR because of the Yalta Conference). This quick shift in perceived enemies would cause problems in holding the Japanese accountable for what they had done. However, the stories of the horrors of the Japanese occupation across Asia would not go completely unpunished. There had been too many witnesses to what had happened in Nanjing for the Japanese military to go entirely free.

Following the Japanese surrender, American troops were sent to Nanjing to restore order as quickly and as safely as possible. They arrived on September 3rd, 1945. The entire airfield where they landed was under

Japanese control. With about fifty Americans and less than three hundred Chinese citizens, they were vastly outnumbered by the seventy thousand Japanese soldiers. These Japanese soldiers had not seen the devastation in their own country, so they were displeased with the orders to lay down their weapons. Still, they would not disobey orders, so the city was fairly quickly occupied by the US. Nanjing was far more organized than Shanghai, which was said to be in chaos following the end of the war. Both cities would soon fall under the control of the Chinese government and the leader of one of the two factions, Mao Zedong. By 1950, most of the foreigners had left Nanjing.

Chapter 17 – The Nanjing War Crimes Tribunal and John Rabe's Life after the Events in Nanjing

As the world looked for answers to how things could have gotten so out of control to result in a second world war, with both Germany and Japan committing some of the worst atrocities in modern memory, the victorious nations began to look to hold people accountable. Just like the Nuremberg trials that sought to hold the German commanders accountable for the Holocaust and other war crimes, the Allies started to put prominent Japanese government officials and military commanders on trial. The events at Nanjing were some of the worst war crimes that the Japanese would be held accountable for after the war ended.

Documentation of the Atrocities

The Westerners in the Safety Zone had documented what they had witnessed during those six weeks in December 1937 and January 1938, with letters, diaries, and pleas to outside nations to intercede. These would again be brought forth, but they were not the only recorded details about that nightmarish time. As mentioned, the Japanese had embedded reporters, as well as the military, who kept their own records. Perhaps the most disturbing part of the records that the Japanese kept were the haunting photographs that showed men standing over their helpless victims as they prepared to execute men who were clearly unarmed. Soldiers posed while holding swords over their victims, whose eyes were usually downcast as they knew what was coming. There are many pictures of the horrific killings, but they did not record the rapes, perhaps knowing just how those photos would be perceived.

These pictures showed a side of the soldiers that would be deemed base instead of glorious. Some Chinese citizens actually got their hands on some of the pictures or the negatives. After making duplicate copies, they then snuck the pictures out of China. This undermined the attempts by the Japanese high command to destroy all of the evidence of what had occurred in the city. As the victorious nations began to prepare to start a trial, the pictures were provided as proof of wrongdoing. These harrowing images would be strong evidence against all levels of the Japanese military because officers and other officials could be easily recognized watching and participating in the war crimes.

Japanese soldiers and officers would eventually speak about what had happened. Some admitted what they had done during the tribunal, while others had kept diaries that were not destroyed by the Japanese government. Over the decades, some would try to atone for what they did, and some of their children would call for a more open discussion about what happened so that people could avoid committing similar crimes in the future.

The International Military Tribunal for the Far East: Determining Who Was Responsible

The US government appointed General Douglas MacArthur to head the occupation of Japan, which took place from 1945 to 1952. Among his responsibilities was to establish a war justice system to try the Japanese for their war crimes. In May 1946, the International Military Tribunal for the Far East was held in Tokyo. By this time, the Nuremberg trials had already established the procedures to be used, so MacArthur and other leaders used this as a template to indict twenty-eight Japanese, which included both members of the military and governmental figures. They were charged with crimes against peace (a charge that included their aggressive invasion of neighboring countries), crimes against humanity, and war crimes. However, there have been many who criticized the small number of Japanese people who ended up facing trial when there were so many more who should have been included. As John Dower would later describe the way people were chosen to be held accountable, the focus was on a few select people. The Japanese military police were not tried, the industrialists who encouraged and profited from the war were not tried, members of secret societies were not tried, and scientists who committed atrocities that rivaled what the Germans had done were not tried. Perhaps the most notable absence, though, was the Imperial family—not even Emperor Hirohito was tried for what his nation had done in his name. The rationale for this came from General MacArthur, who wanted to stabilize the nation as quickly as possible. The US felt the best way to do that was to leave the emperor as the head of the government. The people, particularly soldiers, had acted in his name, so it was hoped that his continued presence as their leader would help the Japanese to accept their defeat and the American occupation. The Far East Tribunal was also not focused solely on what happened in Nanjing, but it was one of the primary events that were scrutinized.

Unlike the Nuremberg trials, the Far East Tribunal was largely trying people for failing to act, known as crimes of omission. General Matsui Iwane and Hirota Koki (the foreign minister when the atrocities occurred) were perhaps the two people most targeted for crimes of omissions, as they had failed to control the soldiers. The prosecution gave evidence that both men knew what was happening in Nanjing but did not take actions to prevent the activities from occurring for far too long. Both men were convicted, with Hirota's judgment being particularly scathing:

> The tribunal is of the opinion that Hirota was derelict in his duty in not insisting before the Cabinet that immediate action be taken to put an end to the atrocities, failing any other action open to him to bring about the same result. He was content to rely on assurances which he knew were not being implemented while hundreds of murders, violations of women, and other atrocities were being committed daily. His inaction amounted to criminal negligence.
>
> - International Military Tribunal for the Far East: Judgement of 4 November 1948

It was much easier to hold General Matsui accountable, as he was the commander of the efforts in Nanjing and had been present for the duration of the atrocities. General Matsui had certainly been the commander of the troops, but he had been too ill to lead them into the city. This does not absolve him of the atrocities, though, as he knew about what was happening and did not stop it. The attacks lasted six weeks, even as the foreigners in the Safety Zone repeatedly asked for intervention. Hirota had been responsible for the response, and he chose to do nothing for more than a month.

All twenty-eight people who were charged were convicted. Seven of them (including Matsui and Hirota) were convicted of the most serious crimes and were sentenced to hang. The other Japanese who were convicted were given jail sentences. Two of the twenty-eight men had died prior to the end of the tribunal, and one was found to be insane.

The seven men were executed on December 23rd, 1948.

There has been a lot of criticism for the trials, especially considering the atrocities that took place in Nanjing. It was felt by critics (especially the Chinese) that not enough people were held accountable, and the trials appeared to be more for show than a way of actually holding the Japanese accountable. The comparable trials against the Germans included 199 defendants and 161 convictions, with 37 criminals receiving a death sentence for their crimes. By comparison, the Japanese seemed to have largely gotten away with some of the worst war crimes in modern history.

This apparent bias was likely a result of the American leaders wanting to start implementing democracy in Japan with minimal resistance. With World War II over, they no longer viewed the Japanese as their enemies; the Chinese and Soviets were. This likely played a significant role in the lack of convictions. They didn't want to alienate the Japanese. Americans also played a large role in establishing education during their occupation, and the atrocities committed by the Japanese were largely omitted from the curriculum.

John Rabe

The role that John Rabe played during the preparation of the Imperial Army's arrival through the post-war events seems to be a contradiction to most people. He had only been in Nanjing to work as a teacher. He worked for the German company Siemens, and by 1931, he was helping to establish phone lines across the city. He and his family lived in a comfortable home that would eventually be located in the Safety Zone. In 1934, Rabe started a German school, which he held in his home. While acting as the chairman of the school board, he became a member of the Nazi Party (he had not lived in Germany since 1908). He would remain faithful to the party throughout the entire war, but it was very likely he had no idea what the party was doing in Europe since he had not been to Germany in decades. He flew the Nazi flag proudly over his home and school and also had a Nazi flag draped over his car. Rabe would have likely been a very easily identifiable figure in the city even before it became clear that a war was coming.

Rabe had chosen to stay in the city and had been instrumental in ensuring that the Safety Zone was established before the Imperial Army arrived. He had actively worked to protect soldiers who sought to hide from the Japanese, especially as it became clear that they would all be executed. Rabe's role in helping the people cannot be overstated, and he seemed to make it his mission to keep the people safe. The correspondence that he sent would be used to help convict Japanese military officials and leaders, even as the Nazi Party was being held accountable for their atrocities in Europe.

Once the Safety Zone was dissolved, the Siemens company told him to return home. They had heard about how he had led the people within the zone, and they may have wanted him to take a leadership role within the company. He did not receive such a role, but he did give lectures about what he had seen, including photographs and films that the Japanese had not managed to take from him. The German Gestapo stopped him when he returned to Berlin, and it was only because of the intervention of

Siemens that he was able to keep his evidence.

When World War II ended, Rabe was denounced for his participation in the Nazi Party. The Soviet enforcement agency called the NKVD arrested him for this. They investigated him, but when that ended, they discharged him. Unfortunately, soon after, he was released, and the British Army arrested him. He went through the same process once again and was eventually discharged. About a year after the war in Europe ended, the Allies declared that he had been successfully "de-Nazified," but he was not given his full pension. The last few years of his life, Rabe was relatively poor, and it was only due to the parcels that the Chinese government sent him, along with some recompense, that he was able to keep going. He died in January of 1949 at the age of sixty-five. He was buried in Berlin, where Germans and Chinese still visit the grave to remember him. His headstone was later moved to the Nanjing Massacre Memorial.

Chapter 18 – The Memorial Hall of the Victims in Nanjing

While the events of that six-week period were well documented, they were largely ignored for decades. However, the Chinese survivors did not forget what had happened. The Nanjing Municipal Government built a memorial for the victims in 1985 in Jiangdongmen (one of the locations where mass executions were carried out and bodies were buried). It was called the Memorial Hall to the Victims in the Nanjing Massacre by Japanese Invaders.

The memorial was expanded in 1995, then again between 2005 and 2007, and today, it includes seventy-four thousand square meters. The outside portion of the memorial has exhibits that reflect the indignation and grief that the period caused, and it includes depictions of both life and death, with statues and carvings depicting the scenes of lost lives among the beautiful cypresses and pines. One of the monuments includes an engraving of the date the Japanese entered the city and the date when they left, at the end of January the following year. Another marble memorial includes some of the names of the victims, as well as the number 300,000, which is one of the most common estimates for the number of Chinese who were killed in Nanjing. Visitors can walk among the outdoor memorials to reflect on how so many people senselessly lost their lives to the invading Japanese army.

The exhibits were divided into three parts: an outdoor exhibit for reflection, the bones of some of the victims, and historical documents from the period.

The bones were excavated from the area when the memorial was made. This part of the exhibit includes coffins in which the bones rest. More than two hundred bones were found during an excavation in 1998. A second area is partially underground and displays roughly one thousand items that recall the tragedies that occurred during that brief period of time. Images taken during the events of that six-week period are displayed on the walls. There are also film documentaries that detailed what life was like for the Nanjing citizens who were trapped within the city.

For the 70th anniversary of the arrival of the Japanese in the city (December 13th, 2007), a new hall was open to the public. This part of the memorial was built to look like a ship's bow, as a way of representing "the Ship of Peace." When a person looks at the new addition in profile, it looks more like a broken saber. When looking directly down at the memorial, it appears to be a sword that transforms into a plowshare.

The purpose of the memorial is to remember those who died and to remind people of what can be done during war and how people who would be reluctant to even kill a snake in their garden back home can be worked into a frenzy. It attempts to educate people, not to sustain animosity toward the nation that perpetrated the crimes but to remind people that they cannot let it happen again. With some people trying to deny that any such event occurred or claiming that it wasn't as bad as the Chinese say, it is a way of showing that the facts were not inventions of anyone's imagination but real accounts of what happened.

Ultimately, the large memorial attempts to remind people that the world is not so far removed from some of the worst atrocities it has seen. It is more about prevention through education, as well as serving as a way of honoring and remembering those who lost their lives.

Chapter 19 – How the Atrocities Were Reported and Resulting Controversies

In the decades since 1938, the Rape of Nanjing has been revisited by survivors, perpetrators, and nations around the world.

How the US Reported the Rape of Nanjing

In the US, the horrors at Shanghai and Nanjing would be used to help stir up sentiment against the Japanese (this happened a few years before Pearl Harbor united the nation against the Axis Powers). Americans lived in Shanghai and Nanjing, and they were among the people who sent word back to their families, the Japanese Embassy, and other governmental figures in the hopes that something would be done to stop the tragedy from unfolding in Nanjing. The American diplomat in the city reported back to the US what he had heard from witnesses. However, it was the American journalists who chose to remain that reported back to news agencies in the US, detailing how the carnage began and was sustained for what felt like forever. The days bled into each other as Japanese soldiers killed indiscriminately, and the screams of women being abducted, raped, and murdered were a constant part of the city's noise.

There were reporters present from several prominent US and British news agencies, such as Archibald Trojan Steele (*Chicago Daily News*), Frank Tillman Durdin (*New York Times*), Arthur von Briesen Menken (Paramount Newsreel), Leslie C. Smith (Reuters), and Charles Yates McDaniel (Associated Press). These five reporters began to send back word of what they saw, though they were unable to send anything during the worst periods of the massacre. Their goal was to let the rest of the world know about the crimes the Japanese were perpetrating as the Second Sino-Japanese War began.

Steele had left Shanghai on the USS *Oahu* and returned to the ship after witnessing the atrocities of those early days. He was able to convince the radio operator on the gunboat to send a cable back to Chicago. On December 15th, 1937, the *Chicago Daily News* broke the story, writing, "Nanking's fall is a story of indescribable panic and confusion among the entrapped Chinese defenders, followed by a reign of terror by the conquering army that cost thousands of lives, many of them innocent ones." This was only two days after the Japanese entered the city, yet their behavior had already horrified those who witnessed it. Menken soon sent his own report to the *Seattle Daily Times* from the same vessel.

The other three journalists found other ways to cable back their own reports to their respective employers. From the very beginning of the atrocities, there were witnesses who reported back to the media, making it impossible for the Japanese to control the narrative around the rest of the world. Some of these reporters would continue to report what they had seen even after leaving Nanjing. Other Americans (not members of any news agency) continued to send reports from within the city as well. As they were unable to leave, they continued to record what they saw, eventually finding ways to get their information out to the world.

Many of the Westerners actually tried to get their reports out, but reports back to Europe were not quite as sensational, as the continent was already tense from Germany's actions during the late 1930s. Some of the stories from the US were reported in Europe. Not all of the reporters were American either, though their stories were printed on several continents.

How Japan Reported the Events of Nanjing

Due to their tight control over the way their soldiers' behavior was reported, the Japanese military and government ensured that none of the atrocities were reported. News of what was unfolding in Nanjing reached Japanese authorities quickly, as the Westerners who had remained sent messages to both the Japanese and their own nations in the hope that someone would end the atrocities.

The soldiers would be too ashamed to talk about what they had done even years after the events. When they did talk, they often seemed detached from the events, as if they knew how they would be judged for their actions.

While the Japanese citizens were aware of the events of the tribunal, the full extent of the war crimes and crimes against humanity were not detailed to them. This would have some serious repercussions later, as Japanese civilians would remain ignorant of the events. Due to this, some would be less willing to believe the recorded details. Similar to how Germans who had not seen the atrocities carried out by the Nazis would not believe reports, the Japanese could not see how their military would do anything so atrocious. The difference was the way that the two Axis Powers would eventually teach their younger generations about World War II. Today, German schools highlight how important it is to remember what they had done so they (or anyone else) would not do it again. By comparison, many Japanese citizens know about the tragedy that occurred in Nanjing, but they don't understand or believe the full scope of what took place. The US did not help, as it failed to take a similar approach as the Germans when it came to teaching the Japanese, even though the US controlled nearly every aspect of Japanese life during the occupation. However, the German curriculum following the war had a lot of input from the nations that Germany had attacked, so it is understandable that they were more transparent and accurate in their portrayal of their role.

The Nazi Party had taken a very similar approach in masking its atrocities, but the two very different approaches to educating future generations would result in two very different perceptions of the war.

Japanese Recognition of Their Crimes

The Japanese government has not entirely faced their history head-on the way the Germans did (though it can be argued that the Germans had a lot more pressure to do so following World War II). Japan did not even publicly acknowledge what had happened until 1972. Prime Minister Tanaka Kakuei issued a statement to the People's Republic of China, saying, "[We are] keenly conscious of the responsibility for the serious damage that Japan caused in the past to the Chinese people through war, and deeply reproaches itself." It was short of an apology and failed to acknowledge any of the events for which Japan was said to reproach itself.

During the 1980s, Emperor Hirohito spoke to South Korean President Chun Doo Hwan, expressing his own personal regret. "It is indeed regrettable that there was an unfortunate past between us for a period in this century and I believe that it should not be repeated again." Later in the year, Japanese Prime Minister Nakasone Yasuhiro would express similar regret for what had happened by "unleashing of rampant ultra-nationalism and militarism and the war that brought great devastation of the people of many countries around the world and to our country as well."

For the 50th anniversary of the start of the war (August 1995), the Japanese prime minister issued Japan's first official statement of regret, saying that the Japanese needed to atone for what it had done in the past. Several more apologies have been issued in the years since, with the most recent being made by Prime Minister Abe Shinzo. With his last apology, Abe expressed a desire to stop apologizing, saying, "We must not let our children, grandchildren, and even further generations to come, who have nothing to do with that war, be predestined to apologize." Following this, he did say that Japanese citizens needed to be aware of their past, even if they shouldn't keep apologizing for it.

Controversies

Just as there are Holocaust deniers today, there are people who deny that the events in Nanjing occurred or that they were not nearly as horrific as some people claim. In addition to some claiming that the images were doctored to make the Japanese look worse, there are claims that the reports about Nanjing were specifically biased against the Japanese. Over the last few decades, deniers have called books and other media that discuss the atrocities as propaganda that are meant to turn people against the Japanese.

While a lot of the film footage and images were authentic, there were some that were doctored or entirely faked by the Chinese and Americans. With there being a reported 200,000 living in Nanjing before the war, the reports of more than 300,000 people being killed are questionable. There were soldiers and other people who sought refuge in the city, but the entire Chinese population in the city was not killed (though a significant portion of the population was killed, as the immediate investigation showed). It is possible that some events of the Nanjing Massacre were exaggerated, but that is the problem. The numbers and a few events may have been exaggerated, but even the Japanese soldiers themselves and their own photographs prove that the atrocities were very real. Too many reports from the neutral Westerners in the city, particularly the pleas from John Rabe himself, showed that it was a nightmarish chapter in the city's history.

The events of Nanjing definitely did happen, but it is also easy to understand the concern that people might be trying to create a wave of anti-Japanese sentiment. During World War II, the US established their own concentration camps for Japanese-Americans; there were no such camps for the Germans. In Europe, the reports from Nanjing made many Europeans very anti-Japanese. This is more a symptom of another problem. Even though the Germans have taught their citizens about the horrors the Nazis committed, the Germans were vilified for decades after World War II. Anything associated with Germans was treated as dangerous. For example, German Shepherds, Doberman Pinschers, and Rottweilers had long been desirable breeds, but this changed after World War II. While they are great guard dogs, their German roots vilified the breeds. They were depicted as dangerous dogs who were more likely to kill people. Because of this, they were (and still are) on banned dog breed lists in different communities around the world. This kind of demonization of a people is not abnormal, as it has happened time and time again in history. Thus, it is easy to understand the concern that detailing atrocities could turn people against an entire nation. There remains a fairly anti-Japanese sentiment in many other Asian nations even today.

However, it is important to take an approach that is similar to the memorial in Nanjing. History should be taught in a way that is both accurate and instructional. It shouldn't be used to justify future atrocities or biases. Denying that something happened is just as harmful as using history to vilify an entire people.

All nations are guilty of atrocities against other groups of people, even today. Accountability and accuracy are important for proper education to prevent similar massacres in the future.

Conclusion

During the Second Sino-Japanese War, Japan attempted to expand its empire across the Asian continent. Like their German allies, the Japanese were experiencing a particularly violent form of nationalism, with many believing that they were superior to all other Asian nations and the Japanese military being particularly insistent that no other nation could defeat them. A lot of this could be attributed to how successful they had been when fighting against China and Russia, and this likely helped them to start viewing people of other nations as being lesser.

Their dehumanization would result in one of the worst atrocities of the war when the Japanese decided to invade Nanjing. As they made their way across the mainland, the Japanese military did not differentiate between the people in the Chinese military and the Chinese citizens. At the time, China's capital was Nanjing, making it an obvious target for a Japanese attack. The Chinese government began an evacuation, getting many of their most important figures out of the city before the Japanese reached it, but many citizens could not escape.

When the Japanese arrived in Nanjing in December 1937, they immediately began a massacre that was unbelievable. The barbarism enacted against the Chinese indicated that the Japanese didn't even see the citizens as people. Lining people up and slaughtering them in a grotesque competition, raping citizens before killing them, looting the homes of the people they killed, and destroying over a third of the city's buildings were some of the most heinous acts of the Japanese military, but there were many other atrocities that they enacted upon the civilians. They branched out to destroy surrounding towns, ensuring that no one would stand against them when they established the city as the capital for their puppet government.

When World War II finally ended, the men who ordered the attacks were tried and convicted of war crimes, but this did not make up for the actions they had done. One of the reasons that the Nanjing Massacre Memorial was created was to remember the lives that were senselessly lost over that six-week period. The atrocities at Nanjing were just as horrific as the tragedies of the Holocaust, but until more recently, it has not been as widely discussed. It is important to remember these kinds of atrocities to help ensure people are aware and so similar atrocities aren't committed in the future.

Here's another book by Captivating History that you might like

Free Bonus from Captivating History (Available for a Limited time)

Hi History Lovers!

Now you have a chance to join our exclusive history list so you can get your first history ebook for free as well as discounts and a potential to get more history books for free! Simply visit the link below to join.

Captivatinghistory.com/ebook

Also, make sure to follow us on Facebook, Twitter and Youtube by searching for Captivating History.

Sources

Auer, James E., and Tsuneo Watanabe. *From Marco Polo Bridge to Pearl Harbor: Who Was Responsible?*. 2006.

Bishop, Chris. *The Encyclopedia of Weapons of World War II*. Sterling Publishing Company, 2002.

Chang, Iris. *The Rape of Nanking: The Forgotten Holocaust of World War II*. Mountain View: Ishi Press, 2012.

Dear, Ian, and Michael R. Foot. *The Oxford Companion to World War II*. New York: Oxford University Press, USA, 2001.

Peattie, Mark, Edward Drea, and Hans V. Ven. *The Battle for China: Essays on the Military History of the Sino-Japanese War of 1937-1945*. 2013.

Spence, Jonathan D. *The Search for Modern China*. New York: W. W. Norton & Company, 1990.

Yoshimi, Yoshiaki. *Grassroots Fascism: The War Experience of the Japanese People*. New York: Columbia University Press, 2015.

[10 Facts about the Second Sino-Japanese War](www.historyhit.com/), Sophie Gee, HistoryHit, October 23, 2020, www.historyhit.com/

A Question of Morality: John Rabe, Facing History and Ourselves, April 11, 2021, www.facinghistory.org/

An Epidemic in Lu Chow Fu – A Glimpse of Mission Work in 1900's China, China Change, February 20, 2012, chinachange.org/2012/02/20/

Brief History of Nanjing, XU Chengyan, ISLS Organizing Committee, March 5, 2017, www.nfls.com.cn/isls/

Bushido: The Ancient Code of the Samurai Warrior, Edward Drea, Greg Bradsher Robert Hanyok, James Lide, Michael Petersen, Daqing Yang, March 22, 2021, Nazi War Crimes and Japanese Imperial Government Records Interagency Working Group, Washington DC, www.archives.gov/

Did It Really Help to Be a Japanese Colony? East Asian Economic Performance in Historical Perspective, Anne Booth, May 2, 2007, The Asia-Pacific Journal, apjjf.org/-Anne-Booth/2418/article.html

First Sino-Japanese War, Editors of Encyclopedia Britannica, Encyclopedia Britannica, March 1, 2021, https://www.britannica.com/event/First-Sino-Japanese-War-1894-1895

How Japan Tried to Save Thousands of Jews from the Holocaust, Kevin McGeary, March 28, 2019, Los Angeles Review of Books China Channel, chinachannel.org/

Iris Chang, *The Rape of Nanking: The Forgotten Holocaust,* December 1991, Basic Books

Japan, China, the United States and the Road to Pearl Harbor, 1937-41, Office of the Historian, Foreign Service Institute, United States Department of State, March 1, 2021, https://history.state.gov/milestones/1937-1945/pearl-harbor

Japanese Crimes in Nanjing, 1937-38: A Reappraisal, Jean-Louis Margolin, OpenEdition Journals. Accessed January 2, 2021, journals.openedition.org/

Japanese Imperialism and the Road to War, Facing History and Ourselves, March 1, 2021, https://www.facinghistory.org/resource-library/teaching-nanjing-atrocities/japanese-imperialism-and-road-war

Nanjing Massacre: Chinese History, The Editors of Encyclopedia Britannica, Britannica, March 2, 2021, www.britannica.com/event/Nanjing-Massacre

Researching Japanese War Crimes, Edward Drea, Greg Bradsher Robert Hanyok, James Lide, Michael Petersen, Daqing Yang, March 22, 2021, Nazi War Crimes and Japanese Imperial Government Records Interagency Working Group, Washington DC, www.archives.gov/

Second Sino-Japanese War, Editors of Encyclopedia Britannica, Encyclopedia Britannica, March 1, 2021, https://www.britannica.com/event/Second-Sino-Japanese-War

Seeds of Unrest: The Taiping Movement, Facing History and Ourselves, March 2, 2021, www.facinghistory.org/nanjing-atrocities/

Shanghai 1937: This Is China's Forgotten Stalingrad, Michael Peck, May 30, 2016, The National Interest, nationalinterest.org/

Sino-Japanese Relations: Issues for U.S. Policy, Emma Chanlett-Avery, Kerry Dumbaugh, William H. Cooper, Congressional Research Service, December 19, 2008, https://fas.org/sgp/crs/row/R40093.pdf

The Marco Polo Bridge Incident, Kallie Szczepanski, November 17, 2019, Thought Co., www.thoughtco.com/

The Nanjing Massacre: A Japanese Journalist Confronts Japan's National Shame, Honda Katsuichi, 1999, M.E. Sharpe, Taylor & Francis

The Nanking Massacre, 1937, Kallie Szczepanski, Thought Co, March 6, 2017, www.thoughtco.com/

The Rape of Nanking or Nanjing Massacre (1937), Historical Work Material, March 3, 2021, www.pacificwar.org.au/

The Story of the Royal Ulster Rifleman and the Battle of Shanghai, History, March 20, 2021, Sky History, www.history.co.uk/

War Zone – City of Terror: The Japanese Takeover of Shanghai, Military History Matters, February 8, 2013, Currently Publishing, www.military-history.org/

What Motivated Japanese Aggression in World War II?, Kallie Szczepanski, July 27, 2019, Thought Co, www.thoughtco.com/

Who Were the Comfort Women? The Establishment of Comfort Stations, Digital Museum, March 22, 2021, Asian Women's Fund, www.awf.or.jp/e1/facts-01.html

Why Japanese Forces Showed "No Mercy" during the Fall of Shanghai, Warfare History Network, May 10, 2020, The National Interest, nationalinterest.org/

The Nanjing Atrocities Reported in the U.S. Newspapers, 1937-38, Suping Lu, April 12, 2021, Readex, www.readex.com/

International Military Tribunal for the Far East: Judgement of 4 November 1948, John Pritchard, Sonia M. Zaide, Vol. 22, April 12, 2021, crimeofaggression.info/documents/6/1948_Tokyo_Judgment.pdf

Memorial Hall to the Victims in the Nanjing Massacre, Travel China Guide, April 8, 2021, www.travelchinaguide.com/

First Battle of Shanghai; 28 Jan 1932 - 8 Mar 1932, C. Pen Chen, March 20, 2021, World War II, ww2db.com/

Second Battle of Shanghai; 13 Aug 1937 - 9 Nov 1937, C. Pen Chen, March 20, 2021, World War II, ww2db.com/

The Shanghai Incident, 1932, PE Matt, February 7, 2015, Pacific Eagles WWII Pacific War Combat, pacificeagles.net/

Samurai and Bushido, History.com Editors, August 21, 2018, History, www.history.com/

Nanking Massacre, History.com Editors, June 7, 2019, History.com, www.history.com/

Japanese War Crimes Trial Begins, History, July 28, 2019, A&E Television Networks, www.history.com/

The First Sino-Japanese War, Kallie Szczepanski, October 17, 2019, Thought Co, www.thoughtco.com/

A Brief History of Manchuria, Kallie Szczepanski, January 5, 2020, Thought Co., www.thoughtco.com/

Credibility and End of the League, The National Archives, March 19, 2021, www.nationalarchives.gov.uk/

Japan-China Friendship Office, Rawfish-Maguro, MIT, March 1, 2021, http://www.mit.edu/course/17/17.s21/maguro.old/friends_home.html

Nanjing History, Travel China Guide, March 1, 2021, www.travelchinaguide.com/

Sino-Japanese War: WW2, Sky History, AE Networks, March 3, 2021, www.history.co.uk/

The Second Sino-Japanese War, Alpha History, March 3, 2021, alphahistory.com/

BRIA 18 3b The "Rape of Nanking," Constitutional Rights Foundation, April 11, 2021, Civics Renewal Network, www.crf-usa.org/bill-of-rights-in-action/

Japanese Invade Manchuria, History Central, March 19, 2021, www.historycentral.com/

Battle of Shanghai, Yuen, Tony, Iris, March 20, 2021, Nanking Massacre: The Untold Story, depts.washington.edu/

The Road to Nanking, Walter Zapotoczny Jr., March 21, 2021, Warfare History Network, warfarehistorynetwork.com/

Wang Ching-wei, Your Dictionary, April 2021, https://biography.yourdictionary.com/

Geneva Conventions: 1864-1977, Malcom Shaw, April 11, 2021, Britannica, www.britannica.com/

Nanking Massacre, Wikipedia, April 11, 2021, www2.gvsu.edu/

Printed in Great Britain
by Amazon